LOCK UP YOUR DAUGHTERS

A Musical Play

Adapted by
BERNARD MILES

From **HENRY FIELDING'S** Comedy
RAPE UPON RAPE

Music by
LAURIE JOHNSON

Lyrics by
LIONEL BART

SAMUEL FRENCH

LONDON

NEW YORK   TORONTO   SYDNEY   HOLLYWOOD

NOTE ON THE PLAY

By BERNARD MILES

I came upon *Rape Upon Rape* quite by accident, while in the midst of a music-hall tour in 1952. I forget what was the actual town, but I was looking round a second-hand bookshop and on the spine of an ancient, calf-bound quarto was the word "Rape". This made an instant appeal and when, upon looking closer, I saw that the full title was "Rape *Upon* Rape", I took the book down and opened it. Its author was the great Henry Fielding and it was first published in 1730.

A quick glance showed its possibilities, and I bought it. From then until 1959, although many other suggestions were made, it remained my top choice for the opening play. But it was Julius Gellner who suggested it should be extensively cut and turned into a musical. Having done some heavy pruning and extensive rearranging I offered it to three well-known lyric writers, but none of them cared for it sufficiently to collaborate. At last, with the time getting short, a mutal friend introduced me to Laurie Johnson, who introduced me to Lionel Bart. They were at the time working on *The Tommy Steele Story*, and had found they worked together very happily. I remember the now celebrated Lionel Bart paying his first visit to Puddle Dock—no fast sports car then, no silk shirts, cashmere jerseys or suède shoes—just a simple working lad keen as mustard to get his feet on to the ladder of stardom, and little realizing how near he was to planting them there.

They got to work, and within a fortnight produced the lyrics and music—with the single exception of the song *The Gentle Art of Seduction*, which was added later in order to make the play a little longer for its once-nightly Australian tour.

The title "Lock Up Your Daughters" came out of the blue. Obviously Rape Upon Rape was the most appealing, but this was considered a little too warm for the City. One day the composer Anthony Hopkins came down to the site to have a look round and I offered him a glass of wine. "No thanks," he said, "I don't drink." I offered him a cigarette—"No thanks, I don't smoke . . . but Lock Up Your Daughters!" A title was found.

LOCK UP YOUR DAUGHTERS

Opened the Mermaid Theatre in the City of London on the 28th May 1959, for a limited run, and played for 330 performances with the following cast of characters:

(in order of their appearance)

STAFF, a constable	Robin Wentworth
A GENTLEMAN	Barry Jackson
WATCHMEN	Michael Hanbury
	Brian Vanden
SQUEEZUM, a corrupt justice	Richard Wordsworth
(from 20th July 1959)	
QUILL, Squeezum's clerk	Harry Locke
MRS SQUEEZUM	Trevor Ray
	Hy Hazell
SOTMORE ⎱ two gallants	Keith Marsh
RAMBLE ⎰	Frederick Jaeger
BRAZENCOURT, an innkeeper	Roger Boston
A WENCH	Sally Adams
POLITIC, a coffee-house politician	John Sharp
HILARET, Politic's daughter	Stephanie Voss
CLORIS, Hilaret's maid	Madeleine Newbury
DABBLE, Politic's friend	Brendan Barry
FAITHFUL, Politic's servant	David Butler
WORTHY, an honest justice	Roy Adams
(from 13th July 1959)	
CAPTAIN CONSTANT, a military gallant	Richard Butler
A SERVANT	Terence Cooper
	Sama Swaminathan

Directed by PETER COE
Designed by SEAN KENNY
Dances arranged by GILBERT VERNON

A revival opened at the Mermaid Theatre on the 17th May 1962. Of the original cast only Hy Hazell appeared in the revival, and during the run she exceeded 1,000 performances as Mrs Squeezum. After three months the new production transferred to Her Majesty's Theatre, and ran in the West End for a further eighteen months.

THE MUSIC

The original orchestration calls for Harpsichord (or Jangle Piano), Double Bass, two Flutes (each doubling Clarinet and Alto Sax), Clarinet (doubling Bass Clarinet and Baritone Sax), Oboe (doubling Cor Anglais), Trumpet, three Horns, Percussion and Harp: a total of twelve instrumentalists.

The composer later re-orchestrated the score for six instrumentalists: Piano/Conductor, Accordian, Double Bass, Flute, Trumpet and Percussion. He also made an arrangement for two-piano accompaniment.

The scores of all three arrangements are available on hire.

For amateur use scores can be hired from Samuel French Ltd.

For professional use scores can only be obtained on hire from Derek Glynne, Silver City House, 62 Brompton Road, Knightsbridge, London, SW3.

The Vocal Score is published and is on sale. It is obtainable from Samuel French Ltd.

ACT I

PROLOGUE

As the OVERTURE *ends, all the characters named in the opening number are in position, perfectly still. They come briefly to life as they are lit, and freeze again when their light has faded out. In the orchestra a bell is chiming.*

A Nightwatchman, STAFF, *enters up* L, *carrying a lantern on a pole. He crosses, and moves down the steps* R *as he sings.*

STAFF (*singing*)   Nine o'clock on a
Fine summer's night, and
ALL'S WELL.

(*A* YOUNG GALLANT, *escorted by two* WATCHMEN, *enters down* L)

(*Moving* C *on stage level; speaking*) One fine upright gentleman taken in for compromising five nice girls and . . .
(*Singing*)   ALL'S WELL.

(*The* YOUNG GALLANT, *under arrest, crosses in front of Staff and exits down* R, *with the two* WATCHMEN)

(*Crossing towards Justice Squeezum's room, speaking*) Here's old Squeezum——

(JUSTICE SQUEEZUM *is discovered seated on a high stool working at his desk; his clerk,* QUILL, *sits in front of and below his employer, on a seat let in to the face of the desk*)

—trying to find out how many fines he's managed to squeeze from those who'd rather pay fines than be taken in for compromising nice young girls. (*He taps a pocket where he keeps the bribes he receives*) I've got my share . . . he wants his'n.

(SQUEEZUM *briefly glances up from his work to nod knowingly at Staff*)

Evening, Mr Squeezum . . .
(*Singing*)   ALL'S WELL.
(*Moving up the steps* L *and glancing towards Mrs Squeezum's boudoir; speaking*) Poor man's got his expenses. Here's his number-one expense——

(MRS SQUEEZUM *is seated at her dressing-table, powdering her nose and preening. She pauses now and then to sip from a glass of cherry brandy that stands amongst the beauty preparations*)

—Missus Squeezum, sitting at her dressing-table, titivating, liquor tippling—(*he mimics her self-appraising glances in the mirror*)—"I look divine tonight" . . . and
(*Singing*)   ALL'S WELL.
(*He moves above Area 5 and looks down into "the Tavern"*)

(SOTMORE *and* RAMBLE *are seated at a rough tavern table, drinking. The wine absorbs* SOTMORE'S *entire attention, but* RAMBLE'S *mind is distracted by the shapely* SERVING WENCH. *The landlord,* BRAZEN-COURT, *supervises with uncouth crudity*)

(*Speaking*) Here's two young blades swilling away the drink as fast as they can take it. They'll end up under the sheets or under the table—either way . . .
(*Singing*)   ALL'S WELL.
(*He moves to the steps* R *and starts to descend*)

(*Under cover of darkness, a* YOUNG MAN *has entered* L *and is now sitting on the stage in great dejection, down* L, *as if chained to the proscenium arch*)

(*Speaking*) Yonder in the dark, dank prison cell, some poor wretch languishing his life away—(*he continues down to stage level and crosses to down* R)—no good telling him . . .
(*Singing*)   ALL'S WELL.

(POLITIC *sits by a table which is piled with newspapers; he reads the newspaper in his hands, checks against the edition which is on his lap, intent and perturbed*)

(*Speaking*) Mister Politic—silly old dodderer—plodding through reams and reams of newsprint. Firmly believing if they say it's so, it *is* so, and . . .
(*Singing*)   ALL'S WELL.
(*He crosses* C *and turns back as the light shines in Hilaret's bedroom*)

(HILARET, *Politic's daughter, is excitedly preparing for a secret tryst. Her maid,* CLORIS, *is helping to make her even more beautiful*)

(*Speaking*) There's his daughter—sweet young Hilaret—planning to elope with a young gallant. If he's half the man she thinks he is——
(*Singing*)   ALL'S WELL.

(*In the distance, another clock begins to chime*)

                        Nine o'clock on a
                        Fine summer's night, and . . .
(*He whispers*)   LOCK UP YOUR DAUGHTERS!

(*All exit except* HILARET *and* CLORIS.
When the LIGHTS *come up on Hilaret's bedroom,* CLORIS *is packing a bag and* HILARET *is seated at the dressing-table, making final preparations for her elopement*)

HILARET. Well, Cloris, this is a mad frolic. I am horridly frightened at the thought of throwing myself into the power of a man.

CLORIS. It's natural to be frightened at first; I was in a little terror myself on my wedding-day. But it all went off before the next morning. A husband, like other bugbears, loses all his horror when once we know him thoroughly.

HILARET. But if he should not prove a good husband.

CLORIS (*moving to her*) Then you must not prove a good wife. If he keeps a mistress, do you keep a lover; if he stays out drinking with his friends at a tavern, do you be merry with your friends at home.

HILARET. You give fine advice indeed!

CLORIS. Upon my word, madam, that was what I followed myself. I had a rogue of a husband who robbed me of all I had, and kept a mistress under my nose. But I was even with him; for it hath ever been my opinion that a husband who is above doing the duties of his office should keep a deputy. (*She returns to finish packing the bag*)

HILARET. But I suppose you'd been in love with your husband?

CLORIS. Why so I was, madam, as long as he deserved it. But love, like fire, naturally goes out when it hath nothing to feed on.

HILARET (*standing*) Well, if it be possible to be assured of a lover's sincerity, I think I may be assured of Constant's.

CLORIS (*closing the bag and turning to her*) Your passion could have been nowhere better fixed. Captain Constant hath all the qualities any woman could desire. He hath youth, beauty, gallantry, constancy, and—as Master Shakespeare says—all the good gifts of nature.

A PROPER MAN   No. 2

(*As the music begins*, HILARET *moves from her bedroom to below Area 5, on stage level.* CLORIS *watches, with some reservations, as* HILARET *sings in ecstatic anticipation*)

HILARET (*singing*) I trust he really is
What I think he is
He *must* be what he seems to be.
I may be wrong,
But he seems
The Proper Man for me.

Yet how can I be sure
Will our love endure?

CLORIS (*following down to stage level, singing*)
> A woman isn't wise to plan,
> Just be content
> With your lot, madam.
> At least you'll have
> A Proper Man!

HILARET.
> He promises to honour
> And cherish me,
> And satisfy my ev'ry need.

CLORIS (*moving towards her*)
> To fulfil this
> Then he is
> A Proper Man indeed!

HILARET (*a shade apprehensively*)
> But what if when we're spoused
> He forgets his vows
> As oft they tell me husbands can?

CLORIS (*alarmed*)
> If there's a doubt
> Better not run out
> To dally with
> Your Proper Man.

HILARET (*crossing back towards her bedroom*)
> Bother the doubt!
> For the handsome lout
> Must surely be a Proper . . .

CLORIS (*following*)   . . . Someone try and stop her!

BOTH (*together*)   Surely he's a Proper Man!

(*When the music ends,* HILARET *and* CLORIS *hastily assume expressions of guileless innocence as they hear* POLITIC *approaching the bedroom. He carries several newspapers*)

POLITIC (*studying the two girls with some suspicion*) What mischief are you hatching, hey? (*With no idea how close he is to the truth*) It is not possible two women should be together without producing a little mischief.

CLORIS. I always thought a man and a woman the more likely to produce a little mischief.

POLITIC. I suppose you will tell my daughter so, too.

HILARET. Indeed, Papa, she need not—for I was always of that opinion.

POLITIC (*moving to her*) "To govern yourself is harder than to govern a kingdom," said an old philosopher, "but to govern a woman is harder than to govern twenty kingdoms."

HILARET (*with feigned impatience*) I wish you'd stop perplexing yourself with kingdoms. I wish you'd mind your own business instead of the public's. I don't understand one word of your politics.

POLITIC. I am very sorry that you don't. A newspaper would be more profitable for you than a romance. You might learn more from one half-sheet than—(*indicating Cloris*) in all the tittle-tattle of that saucy wretch.

HILARET. I read the gossip paragraphs in the *Whitehall Evening Post*.

POLITIC. If you would be informed in these matters, you must read all that come out. About forty every day—and, some days, fifty. And, of a Saturday, about four-score. Continue on such a course but one twelve-month, and you might know as much of politics as any man at our coffee-house. And I had rather see you a politician than a woman of quality.

HILARET. If I may speak freely, it would have been better for me if you had been less a politician.

POLITIC. Then there you are deceived, very much deceived. You may live to see me one of the greatest men in England.

(CLORIS *crosses to Hilaret and whispers a hurried reminder that valuable time is passing away*)

(*Continuing his "oration", too absorbed in his topic to notice that the girls are hardly paying attention*) At the time of the siege of Gibraltar, did I not say that, within three years, there would be either peace or war? And was I not proved right? And yet I am an ignoramus—I know nothing. (*He turns to the girls, who start guiltily apart*) Hark ye, I am even now contriving a method to pay off the national debt, without a penny of money.

HILARET (*wide-eyed with pretended wonder*) And how is that to be compassed, pray?

POLITIC. Why, by building a machine to carry ships by land, and so prevent the expense of sailing 'em. (*Elated at this master-stroke, he begins to return to his parlour*)

HILARET (*calling after him*) I wish you every success, sir. But now I must take my leave of you, for it grows very late. So, good night, Papa.

POLITIC (*turning to call back*) Good night, my dear.

EXIT MUSIC   No. 2A

(CLORIS *watches to make certain that Politic is safely out of sight, then signals to* HILARET *to hurry. Together, they silently make good their escape from the house. The incidental music fades as* POLITIC *speaks*)

POLITIC (*seated by his table, studying a newspaper*) I cannot rest for these preparations of the Turks. What can be their design? It must be against Austria. Ay, ay, we shall have another campaign in the Balkans. Well, I hope we may feel no other effect from them. Should the Turkish galleys once find a passage through the Straits, who can tell the consequence? I hope I shan't live to see that day.

ENTRANCE MUSIC No. 2B

(DABBLE *enters in great alarm, waving a handful of the latest editions. He is Politic's close friend, and a fellow coffee-house politician*)

DABBLE. We are all undone, neighbour Politic! All blown up! All ruined!

POLITIC. Protect us! What is the matter? No news of the Turks, I hope!

(*Politic's servant,* FAITHFUL, *enters and makes his weary way to Hilaret's bedroom. He is a very old man, and does not hear as well as he used to—but he can still see, and is upset at finding the bedroom deserted*)

DABBLE. The latest edition has an account of the Dauphin's death. (*He shows the paper to Politic*)

POLITIC. Worse and worse! This is a finishing stroke, indeed!

(FAITHFUL *begins his decrepit descent to the parlour*)

Mr Dabble, I take this visit exceeding kind. Pray be pleased to sit. We must confabulate on this important accident.

(DABBLE *sits beside the table*)

Pray light your pipe. I only hope this may not prevent the introduction of Don Carlos into Italy.

(FAITHFUL *has reached the parlour and stands behind Politic's chair, trying vainly to attract his attention*)

FAITHFUL. Sir, sir, Miss Hilaret has gone out of the house and nobody knows whither.

(*But* POLITIC *and* DABBLE *are too concerned with the woes of the world to pay attention*)

DABBLE. I hope so, too! The prospect of affairs in the West is so black, that I see no reason to regard the East. I would fain ask one question, Mr Politic. Pray, how large do you take Tuscany to be?

(POLITIC *pauses for a moment*)

FAITHFUL (*eagerly seizing the opportunity*) Sir, sir, Miss Hilaret has gone out of the house——

POLITIC. How large do I take Tuscany to be?

FAITHFUL. —and nobody knows whither.

POLITIC. Let me see, . . . Tuscany. . . . Aye. How large do I take it to be? (*A desperate guess*) Why, sir, I take it to be about as large as the kingdom of France, or something larger.

DABBLE (*full of scorn*) As large as the kingdom of France? You might as well compare this tobacco pipe to a cannon! Why, Tuscany's only a town.

POLITIC. Allow me to convince you of your error, sir. (*He turns to Faithful*)

FAITHFUL. Sir, Miss Hil . . .

POLITIC. Faithful, bring me Europe hither.

DABBLE. I did not think, Mr Politic, you had been so ignorant of geography.

POLITIC (*offended*) I believe, sir, I know as much as you.

FAITHFUL (*trying again*) Sir, your daughter has gone out of the house, and nobody knows whither!

POLITIC (*to Dabble*) And pray give me leave to tell you, sir, I wish your own ignorance in public affairs doth not appear to our cost.

DABBLE. Sir, I wish you would send for the map.

POLITIC. Map me no map, sir! My head is a map. A map of the entire world. (*Angrily, he snatches another newspaper from the table and studies it*)

DABBLE (*losing his temper*) If your head is a map, sir, it is a very erroneous one.

FAITHFUL (*desperately*) Sir, your daughter has gone out of the house and nobody knows whither!

POLITIC (*discovering a news item*) Great news, Mr Dabble, great news!

DABBLE (*still rather peevish*) More deaths?

POLITIC. No! The Dauphin is alive after all!

DABBLE (*his good humour returning abruptly*) Is there confirmation? Is it certain? (*He leans over to read the newspaper*)

POLITIC (*triumphantly*) Very certain—Stop Press! (*He leans towards Dabble, showing him the paper*)

DABBLE. This is great news, indeed! Great news!

POLITIC. Yes, this news makes me the happiest creature living.

FAITHFUL (*beginning to lose patience, and pushing his head between theirs*) I wish, sir, my news may not prevent it. Your daughter, sir, is gone out of the house, and no-one knows whither.

POLITIC (*registering at last*) My daughter gone! That is some check to my happiness, I confess. But the recovery of the Dauphin would balance the loss of twenty daughters.

(FAITHFUL *gives up in despair, and wanders off, mumbling to himself*)

DABBLE. Yes! Be not concerned at anything, after that splendid news!

IT MUST BE TRUE   No. 3

(*The music begins and, as one man,* DABBLE *and* POLITIC *each choose a fresh newspaper from the pile on the table, and study them closely*) DABBLE (*looking up, singing*)

> It must be true,
> For I read it in the papers, didn't you?

POLITIC (*looking up, singing*)
> It must be true,
> Very revolutionary point of view.

BOTH (*together*)   Tho' the *Evening Post*
> And the *West Gazette*
> Disagree with most
> Of the rest—why fret?

(*They leave their seats and move to* C *stage*)

> It must be true
> Or the editors are in a pretty stew!

DABBLE.   War is much nearer than you think,
POLITIC.   We're standing right upon the brink,
DABBLE.   All through the rising cost of drink,
POLITIC.   Our fleet is liable to sink!

(*They dance a few sedate steps, as they sing*)

DABBLE.   It must be true,
> For I read it in the papers, didn't you?

POLITIC.   It must be true
> Give the credit where the credit's really due.

DABBLE.

If they tell, as fact,
In the *Scotch Dispatch*
How a Pterodactyl's
About to hatch

BOTH (*together*)

It must be true
Study closely and you're sure to find a clue.

(*Dancing triumphantly, newspapers in hand*)

There it is in Black and White,
They insist their facts are right,
How can we pooh-pooh it?
If they say it's true, it
MUST BE TRUE.

(*In a few steps, they collect newspapers from the table and return c with more irrefutable evidence*)

DABBLE.

It must be true,
For I read it in the papers, didn't you?

POLITIC.

It must be true,
It's amazing all the things I never knew!

DABBLE.

If the papers reckon,
And they have sworn,
Ev'ry other second
A baby's born,

BOTH (*together*)

It must be true—
But it must be very difficult to do!

POLITIC.   See here, there's trouble with the Turks,
DABBLE.   Two Scotsmen sat upon their dirks.
POLITIC.   Help wanted in the waterworks
DABBLE.   Precisely where the danger lurks!

BOTH (*together*)

It must be true,
For I read it in the papers, didn't you?

It must be true,
Very revolutionary point of view.

Tho' the *Evening Post*
And the *West Gazette*
Disagree with most
Of the rest—why fret?

It must be true,
Or the editors are in a pretty stew.

Now we know the latest news,
We must go and change our views.

DABBLE.   This new supposition,
POLITIC.   'Til the next edition
BOTH (*together*) MUST BE TRUE.

EXIT MUSIC   No. 3A

(*During the exit music,* DABBLE *goes off and* POLITIC *returns to his seat in the parlour. When the lights have faded on the parlour,* POLITIC *exits under cover of darkness.*

The lights come up on the Tavern in Area 5. RAMBLE, SOTMORE, *and the* SERVING WENCH *have returned to much the same positions they were in during the opening song.* BRAZENCOURT *is just lumbering his way back on stage with a fresh bottle. Almost at once,* RAMBLE *takes the* WENCH *firmly by the wrist and leads her off stage. It is a few seconds before* SOTMORE *misses them*)

SOTMORE (*calling after him in disgust*) Ramble!

(BRAZENCOURT *gives Sotmore a toothless, lascivious leer as he delivers the new bottle*)

(*Unburdening his heart to the audience*) After only two bottles, to sneak away to some beastly little wench! Confound them, they have spoiled so many of my companions—and forced me to bed sober at three o'clock in the morning so often—that if the whole sex were to go to the devil I would drink a bumper to their good journey. (*He illustrates his boast, taking a good pull at his wine*)

(*The* WENCH *returns, giggling, hotly pursued by* RAMBLE, *who hears the last few words of Sotmore's speech*)

RAMBLE. And I would go thither along with them, the dear, charming creatures.

(BRAZENCOURT *cuffs the* WENCH *for deserting her post, and packs her off stage. She glances back at Ramble, who blows her a kiss as she leaves.* BRAZENCOURT *ponderously follows the girl*)
Woman! It is the most wonderful word that ever was invented. There's music, there's magic in it!

(SOTMORE *rises, looking slightly bilious at his friend's misplaced enthusiasm, and joins Ramble down* C)

Mark Anthony knew how to lay out his money when he gave the world for a woman.

SOTMORE. If he'd given it for a hogshead of good claret, I would have commended the purchase more.

RAMBLE. Wine is only the prologue to love; it only serves to raise our expectations. The bottle is but a passport to the bed of pleasure.

SOTMORE (*leading Ramble back to the table*) Before I go into a tavern again with a man who will sneak away after the first bottle, may I be cursed with a pint of beer as long as I live. I'd sooner drink weak tea with a politician than thus be made a whetstone of—to sharpen my friend's inclinations so that some little doxie may enjoy the benefit of the good humour which I have helped to raise. (*He helps himself to more wine, and pours some for Ramble*)

RAMBLE. Why, Sotmore, thou art as peevish as a woman, disappointed in the last moment, when her expectations were at the highest.

SOTMORE (*handing Ramble the wine*) And have I not good cause?

RAMBLE (*raising the mug*) One bottle more, and I had been fit for no company at all. (*He drinks*)

SOTMORE. Then thou hadst been carried off with glory. An honest fellow should no more quit a tavern while he can stand than a soldier should the field. (*He drinks*) But you fine gentlemen are all for preserving yourselves safe from the field and the tavern for the benefit of the ladies.

RAMBLE (*setting down his mug and rising*) Be not so enraged. I'll take but one refreshing turn, and come back to thee. Burgundy shall be the word, and I will fight under thy command till I drop.

SOTMORE. Now thou art an honest fellow—and thou shalt toast whomsoever thou pleasest.

(RAMBLE *goes to follow the direction taken by the* WENCH)

We'll bumper up her health, till thou dost enjoy her in imagination —which shall throw into your arms the soberest prude or the wildest coquette in town.

RAMBLE (*pausing and turning back to Sotmore*) What a luscious picture thou dost draw! But how can imagination provide better bedfellows than the ones I have already known!

RED WINE AND A WENCH   No. 4

RAMBLE (*singing*)   I dallied long with Marguerite—
Soft as a swan and, ah, so sweet!
Now she's absconded with half the Fleet!
Farewell, Marguerite!

	A wench!
SOTMORE (*singing*)	Red wine!
RAMBLE.	A wench!
SOTMORE.	Red wine!
RAMBLE.	Is there anything as comely as
	A wench?
SOTMORE.	Red wine!

(RAMBLE *moves lithely down* c, *bringing Sotmore with him*)

SOTMORE.	Oh, what an inn—the *Prince Connaught*,
	I used to sink or swim in port.
	When I came up, it was up in court;
	Not the *Prince Connaught*.

RAMBLE.	A wench?
SOTMORE.	Red wine!
RAMBLE.	A wench
SOTMORE.	Red wine!
RAMBLE.	Is there anything as comely as
	A wench!
SOTMORE.	Red wine!

RAMBLE.	I'm puzzled by Patricia
	Is she a whore, or is she a
	Regular for the mil-ish-i-a?
	Brave Patricia!

	A wench!
SOTMORE.	Red wine!
RAMBLE.	A wench!
SOTMORE.	Red wine!
RAMBLE.	Is there anything as comely as
	A wench . . . ?

SOTMORE (*joining in*) —Quench your thirst with a hogshead of wine.

RAMBLE.	And a wench!

SOTMORE.	Customers in *The Volunteer*
	Must have been very fond of beer.
	Caught drinking port you'd be
	Thought quite queer!
	In *The Volunteer*.

RAMBLE.	A wench!
SOTMORE.	Red wine!
RAMBLE.	A wench!

Sotmore.	Red wine!
Ramble.	A wench!
Sotmore.	Red wine!
Ramble.	A wench!
Sotmore.	Red wine!
Ramble.	A wench!
Sotmore.	Red wine!
Ramble.	A wench!
Sotmore.	Red wine!
Ramble.	Is there anything as comely as A wench . . . ?

Sotmore (*joining in*) —Quench your thirst with a hogshead of wine.

Ramble.   And a wench!

(*As the music ends,* Sotmore *returns to the tavern table*)

Sotmore. I'll order a new recruit upon the table, and expect thee with impatience.

(*In eager pursuit of some new amorous adventure,* Ramble *waves farewell to Sotmore, and exits. As the lights fade on the tavern,* Sotmore *resumes drinking alone.* Ramble *re-enters, down stage. He is now "in the street outside the Tavern". As the scene proceeds,* Sotmore *exits under cover of darkness*)

Ramble (*ruefully amused at his friend's alcoholic devotion*) Sure, the fellow's whole sensation lies in his throat, for he is never pleased but when he is swallowing! And yet the hogshead will be as soon drunk with the liquor it contains as he with what he drinks. Oh, I wish it had no other effect upon me. Pox on my paper soul! I have no sooner buried the wine in my belly than its spirit rises to my head. I am in a very proper humour for a frolic. If my good genius—and her evil one—would but send me some lovely female in my way . . . !

(*There is the sound of a scuffle, off stage*)

Hey! Hello! (*Moving towards the noise*) The devil hath heard my prayers.

(Hilaret *hurries on, flustered and upset*)

Hilaret. Was ever anything so unfortunate? To lose my maid in a scuffle, and not know a step of the way.

Ramble (*in the shadows*) By all my love of glory, an adventure!

Hilaret (*hearing his voice; alarmed*) Ha! Who's that?

(Ramble *steps forward*)

Who are you, sir?

RAMBLE (*bowing, then moving closer to her*) A cavalier, madam; a knight-errant, rambling about the world in search of adventures. To plunder widows and to ravish virgins.

HILARET (*a trifle haughty, turning away*) I wish you all the success so worthy an adventurer deserves.

RAMBLE. But hold, madam; I am but just now sallied forth, and you are the first adventure I have met with. (*He goes to embrace her*)

HILARET. Let me go, I beseech you, sir. I will have nothing to say to any of your profession. (*She struggles free*)

RAMBLE (*amused at what he takes to be mock modesty*) That's unkind, madam. For, as I take it, our professions are pretty nearly allied.

HILARET (*shocked, and turning on him*) My profession, sir?

RAMBLE. Yes, madam. I believe I am no stranger to the honourable rules of your order. I have only been in the town a week and have already met half a dozen!

HILARET. Nothing but your drink, sir, and ignorance of my quality could excuse such rudeness! (*She turns to go*)

RAMBLE (*catching her, and drawing her back to him*) Why! The daughter of some person of rank, I'll warrant her! Look you, my dear, I shan't trouble myself with your quality. I have had as much joy in the arms of an honest boatswain's wife as with the second cousin of the Lord Chamberlain.

HILARET (*realizing struggle is unavailing, and deciding to try sweet reason and flattery*) You look, sir, so much like a gentleman that I am persuaded this usage proceeds only from your mistaking me.

(*Off guard at this change of tactics,* RAMBLE *lets her go*)

(*Turning to him to continue her reasoning*) I own it looks a little odd for a woman of virtue to be found alone in the street at this hour——

RAMBLE. It does look a little odd, indeed!

HILARET. —but when you know my story I am confident you will assist me, rather than otherwise. I have this very night escaped, with my maid, from my father's house; and, as I was going to put myself into the hands of my lover, a scuffle happening in the street. And my maid and I running away in fright to avoid it, we unluckily separated from each other. Now, sir, I rely on your generosity to assist an unhappy woman—for which you shall have not only my thanks, but those of my lover into the bargain.

RAMBLE (*sarcastically, the prospect not appealing*) I am your lover's humble servant; but I find I am too much in love with you myself to preserve you for another. Had you proved what I at first took you for, I should have parted with you easily. But now I see a coronet in your eyes. (*Aside*) She shall be "Her Grace" if she pleases.

HILARET (*aside*) This is the maddest fellow. I see there is only one way to deal with him—and that is to humour him.

RAMBLE (*returning to her and tenderly playing the part he believes is expected of him*) So, my dear, whether you be of quality or no quality, you and I will go drink one bottle together at the next tavern. (*He takes her hand*) Come, my angel. Oh, this dear soft hand!

HILARET. Could I but be assured that my virtue would be safe!

RAMBLE. Nowhere safer! I'll give thee anything in pawn for it—except my watch.

HILARET. And my reputation?

RAMBLE. The night will take care of that! (*Aside*) Virtue and reputation, egad! This trade has learnt a strange language since I left England!

HILARET (*humouring him*) But will you love me always?

RAMBLE (*with histrionic sincerity*) Oh, for ever and ever!

HILARET. But will you, too?

RAMBLE. Yes, I will, too!

HILARET. And will you promise to be civil?

RAMBLE. Oh, yes! Yes! (*Aside*) I was afraid she would have asked me for money!

HILARET. Then I will venture. Go you into the tavern, and I'll follow you.

(RAMBLE *stops in his tracks. Did she really think he would be taken in by so simple a ploy? He looks at her and laughs knowingly. Since the trick has failed,* HILARET *decides the best thing to do is laugh back at him*)

RAMBLE. Excuse me, madam. I know my duty better. So, if you please, I'll follow you!

HILARET (*braving it out*) No, no! I insist on your going first!

RAMBLE. And so you'll leave me in the lurch. I see you are but frightened at the roughness of my dress, but, foregad, I am an honest tar, and the devil take me if I fail you.

(HILARET *is still hesitant*)

(*Moving as if to pick her up in his arms and carry her*) Nay, if you insist on the ceremony of being carried, with all my heart . . .

HILARET (*hastily moving out of reach*) Nay, sir, do not proceed to rudeness!

'TIS PLAIN TO SEE   No. 5

HILARET (*singing*)	'Tis plain . . .
RAMBLE (*singing*)	What does she say?
HILARET.	. . . to see
RAMBLE.	Come, what act is this?
HILARET.	A girl . . .
RAMBLE.	Is it a play?

HILARET.	. . . like me
RAMBLE.	She must practise this!
HILARET.	Could never be So bo-o-o-o-old.
RAMBLE.	Bo-o-o-o-old.
HILARET.	I am . . .
RAMBLE.	Does she confess?
HILARET.	. . . a maid
RAMBLE.	Thunder strike me down!
HILARET.	Who has . . .
RAMBLE.	Nevertheless——?
HILARET.	. . . not strayed
RAMBLE.	Now she's on the town!
HILARET.	. . . from Doing as I'm to-o-o-o-old.
RAMBLE.	We're to-o-o-o-old.
HILARET.	Innocence is here for all to see.
RAMBLE.	Sin is lurking there as well—
HILARET.	Win a smile from me but no more,
RAMBLE.	Not one . . .
HILARET.	No, sir,
RAMBLE.	. . . little . . .
HILARET.	No more,
RAMBLE.	. . . squeeze?
HILARET.	You must . . .
RAMBLE.	Must we indeed?
HILARET.	. . . agree
RAMBLE.	Yes, we're all agreed
HILARET.	My purity
RAMBLE.	Hey-day—
HILARET.	Is plain . . .
RAMBLE.	It could not
HILARET.	. . . to . . .
RAMBLE.	Be more plain to . . .
BOTH (*together*)	. . . see.

(*The music continues liltingly, and they dance*)

HILARET.	You must . . .
RAMBLE.	Must we indeed?

HILARET.	. . . agree
RAMBLE.	Yes, we're all agreed
HILARET.	My purity
RAMBLE.	Hey-day—
HILARET.	Is plain . . .
RAMBLE.	It could not
HILARET.	. . . to . . .
RAMBLE.	Be more plain to . . .
BOTH (*together*)	. . . see.

(*When the music ends, RAMBLE feels that he has carried the charade far enough*)

RAMBLE. My passion will be dallied with no longer. I have only just come on shore—seen nothing but men and clouds this half year. My stomach's sharp, and you are a tasty dish. If I do not eat you up, may salt beef be my fare for ever. (*He takes her in his arms*)

HILARET (*struggling*) I'll call the watch!

RAMBLE. Nay! If you don't consent, I'll ravish you without!

HILARET (*thoroughly frightened, and calling at the top of her voice*) Help, there! A rape! A rape!

RAMBLE. Hush, hush. You call too loud. People will think you are in earnest.

HILARET. Help! A rape! A rape! A rape!

(*STAFF and the TWO WATCHMEN hurry on*)

STAFF. That's he there! Seize him!

(*RAMBLE lets go of Hilaret and attempts to defend himself against the Watchmen, but he is soon overpowered. The WATCHMEN stand either side of him, pinning his arms. STAFF brings the lantern closer to examine his latest victim*)

RAMBLE. Stand off, ye scoundrels!

STAFF. It's you who should have stood off, sir. (*Turning to Hilaret*) Do you charge this man with a rape, madam?

HILARET. I am frightened out of my senses.

STAFF. It's a plain case! The rape is sufficiently proved. (*He turns to browbeat Ramble, hoping to push up the value of a forthcoming bribe*) What? Was the devil in you, to ravish a woman in the street thus?

RAMBLE. Me? Nay! Mr Constable, I charge that lady with threatening to swear a rape against me, and laying violent hands upon me—while I was inoffensively walking along the street.

HILARET (*aghast*) How, villain!

RAMBLE. The laws are come to a fine pass, truly, when a sober gentleman can't walk the street for women!

HILARET. For heaven's sake, sir, don't believe him.

STAFF. Nay, madam, as we have but a bare affirmation on both sides, we cannot tell which way to incline our belief.

HILARET. This is the most unfortunate accident, sure, that ever befell a woman of virtue.

STAFF. If you are a woman of virtue, the gentleman will be hanged for attempting to rob you of it. If you are not a woman of virtue, you will be whipped for accusing a gentleman of robbing you of what you no longer had to lose. (*He signals to Hilaret that she must join Ramble, under arrest*)

'TIS PLAIN TO SEE (*Reprise*)   No. 5A

(last 9 Bars)

HILARET (*singing*)	You must . . .
RAMBLE WATCHMEN } (*singing*)	Must we indeed?
HILARET.	. . . agree
MEN.	Yes, we're all agreed
HILARET.	My purity
MEN.	Hey-day—
HILARET.	Is plain . . .
MEN.	It could not
HILARET.	. . . to . . .
MEN.	Be more plain to . . .
ALL (*together*)	. . . see.

(*They all exit*, R.
    Under cover of darkness, JUSTICE SQUEEZUM *and* QUILL *have taken their respective positions at the desk in Area 3*. SQUEEZUM *is working industriously at his ledgers*. QUILL *is dozing*)

SQUEEZUM. Did Mother Bilkum refuse to pay my demands?

(*There is no response*. QUILL *dozes on*)

(*Leaning forward and prodding the pen into Quill's wig; much louder*) Did Mother Bilkum refuse to pay my demands?

(QUILL *comes to. His expression suggests that, when it comes to working as Justice Squeezum's clerk, the first forty years are the worst*)

QUILL. Yes, sir; yes, sir. (*Very correct, but relishing his bad tidings*) She says she doesn't value your worship's protection at a farthing; for she can bribe two juries a year to acquit her for half the money she's paid you in the last three months.

SQUEEZUM (*controlling incipient apoplexy at the last moment*) I'll show her I understand something about juries as well as herself. Make a memorandum against her trial—that we be sure to have jury number three. They are a set of good men and true, and hearken to no evidence but mine.

(QUILL *resumes his seat and takes note of the directive*)

And, Quill, d'ye hear?

(QUILL *lifts his head and listens with an air of long-suffering endurance*)

Look out for a new recruit for jury number one. We shall have a swinging vacancy there, next sessions, I fear.

QUILL (*with a sigh*) That jury hath been particularly unfortunate. That's the third good man we've lost this year.

SQUEEZUM (*returning to his work*) We must all take our chance, Quill. The man who would live in this world must not fear the next.

(STAFF *enters*)

Well, Constable?

STAFF. An't please, your worship, we have been to the gaming-house in the alley, and have taken four prisoners, whereof we discharged two that had your worship's licence.

SQUEEZUM. What are the other two?

STAFF. One is a half-pay officer, the other an attorney's clerk.

SQUEEZUM (*ruefully*) Discharge 'em. There is nothing to be gained from the army or the law. The one hath no money, and the other won't part with it.

STAFF. And we've been to the house where your Worship commanded us, and heard the rattle of the dice from the street. But there were two coaches with coronets on them at the door, so we thought it proper not to go in.

SQUEEZUM. You did right. The laws are turnpikes—only made to stop those who travel on foot and not to interrupt those who drive through them in their coaches.

STAFF. And we've taken up a man for rape.

SQUEEZUM (*cheering up at once*) Oh, who's he?

STAFF. I fancy he's some great man, for he talks French, sings Italian and swears English.

SQUEEZUM. Is he rich?

STAFF. We can't get a farthing out of him.

SQUEEZUM (*with enthusiasm*) A sure sign he is! Deep pockets are like deep streams . . .

(QUILL *has heard this particular snippet of wisdom a thousand times before. With an expression of weary resignation he mouths the words as Squeezum speaks, being able to give an accurate forecast of the Justice's forthcoming phrase*)

SQUEEZUM ⎫
QUILL   ⎬ (*together*) { . . . and money, like water, never runs
                                    faster than in the shallows.

STAFF. Then there's another misfortune.

SQUEEZUM. What's that?

STAFF. The woman won't swear against him.

SQUEEZUM. Never fear that. I'll make her swear enough for my purpose. What sort of woman is she?

STAFF. A common harlot.

SQUEEZUM. The properest person in the world to swear a rape. A modest woman is as shy of swearing a rape as a gentleman is of admitting committing one. Bring them before me.

(*He waves the pen airily in Quill's direction and* QUILL *resignedly rises and follows* STAFF *off*)

STAFF (*as he goes*) Yes, your Honour.

(*When they have gone,* SQUEEZUM *works on alone for a few seconds. Suddenly, his wife's voice hails him from off stage and he starts guiltily*)

MRS SQUEEZUM (*off*) Mr Squeezum!

(*She sweeps on stage, and down* C)

I desire, Mr Squeezum, you should finish all your dirty work soon, for I am resolved to have the house to myself this evening.

SQUEEZUM (*clambering down from his desk and joining her*) You shall, my dear. And I shall be obliged to you if you can let me have the coach.

MRS SQUEEZUM. I shall be using it myself.

SQUEEZUM. Then I must get horses put into the chariot.

MRS SQUEEZUM. I am not yet determined whether I shall use the coach or the chariot—so it is impossible you should have either.

SQUEEZUM. Very well. Then I shall only beg the favour of supping a little sooner than ordinary.

MRS SQUEEZUM. That is so far from being possible that we cannot sup until an hour later than usual, because I must attend at an auction, or I shall lose a little china basin, which I may get for not above one hundred guineas. And those guineas, you must give me, honey. (*She holds out her hand*)

SQUEEZUM (*his smile slipping*) A hundred guineas—for a china basin?

MRS SQUEEZUM (*with nonchalance*) I may get it for less. But it is better to have too much money about one than too little.

SQUEEZUM (*determined to be firm this time*) I cannot support your extravagance.

MRS SQUEEZUM (*suddenly with claws*) Now, hark ye, my dear. If, whenever I ask for a trifle, you object to my extravagance, I'll be reveng'd. I'll blow you up. I'll discover all your midnight intrigues, your bribing juries, your supporting ill houses, your whole train of rogueries. (*Sweet reason again*) If you don't give me what I want, honey.

SQUEEZUM (*subsiding as usual*) Well, my dear, this time you shall be indulged.

(SQUEEZUM *takes a leather pouch from his desk and is about to count out the money when* MRS SQUEEZUM, *with an angelic smile, holds out her hand.* SQUEEZUM *shrugs and gives her the pouch intact.* MRS. SQUEEZUM *exits, in seraphic triumph*)

Trust a thief or a lawyer with your purse . . . a physician with your constitution . . . (*shaking his head sadly at the wicked ways of the world*) but never trust a secret with your wife!

ON THE SIDE   No. 6

SQUEEZUM (*singing*)

> Tho' your wife is yours
>   To have and to hold, sir,
> Do anything but in her confide.
> Be secret and deep
> And keep what you'd keep
> On the Side!
> On the Side!
>
> You must lead her to
>   Believe she can trust you
> And never let her see that you've lied
> When she's not in view,
> Who cares what you do?
> Be secret and deep
> And keep what you'd keep
> On the Side!
> On the Side!
>
> When you're sitting on
>   The Bench in the Courtroom
> You double all the fines to provide
> A trifle for your purse
> Which your wife will not disburse.
> When she's not in view
> Who cares what you do?
> Be secret and deep
> And keep what you'd keep
> On the Side!
> On the Side!

> You must get the most
>   You can out of Justice;
> And "Justice" is a term which is wide.
> A misguided girl to judge,
> With a shapely shape to nudge,
> Or a trifle for your purse
> Which your wife'll not disburse
> When she's not in view
> Who cares what you do?
> Be secret and deep
> And keep what you'd keep
> On the Side!
> On the Side!
>   (*He dances a few steps*)
> (*Whispering*)   On the Side! (*He returns to his desk*)

(*As the music ends, with a loud chord,* STAFF *and the* WATCHMEN *return, bringing* RAMBLE *and* HILARET *with them*)

STAFF. An't please, your Worship, here is the gentleman that committed a rape on this young woman.

SQUEEZUM. Bring 'em before me. (*He glances at Hilaret for the first time, and is at once deeply impressed*) Hath he indeed ravished you, child?

HILARET. Sir, I have nothing to say against him. I desire you would give us both our liberty. He was a little frolicsome, which made me call for these people's help. And when once they had taken hold of us, they would not suffer us to go away.

SQUEEZUM. Oh, they did their duty. The power of discharging lieth in us, not in them.

RAMBLE. Sir . . .

SQUEEZUM (*at once, and fiercely*) Sir, I beg we may not be interrupted. (*Cooing again*) Hark ye, young woman, if this fellow hath treated you in an ill manner, do not let your modesty prevent the execution of Justice.

(STAFF *signals to the* WATCHMEN, *who turn and exit*)

HILARET. Sir, I assure you he is innocent.

SQUEEZUM. Mr Staff, what say you to this affair?

STAFF. And it please your Worship, I saw the prisoner behaving in a very indecent manner, and heard the young woman say he hath ravished away her senses.

SQUEEZUM. Fie upon you, child. Will you not swear to this?

HILARET. No, sir. But I will swear something against you unless you discharge us.

SQUEEZUM. Very well, if you will not swear, the prisoner shall remain in custody till you will.

STAFF. We can swear enough to convict him.

SQUEEZUM (*to Ramble*) I never saw such a ravishing look in all my life. Sir, I've a mind to hang you without any evidence at all. 'Tis such fellows as you who sow dissension between man and wife and people the world with little bastards.

(MRS SQUEEZUM *enters and moves down the steps nearest to her boudoir, to stage level*)

RAMBLE. Nay, if that be all you accuse me of, I confess it freely. I have employed my time pretty well. Though I cannot see why you should be so incensed against me; for I do not imagine you to be a very great enemy to these amusements.

(JUSTICE SQUEEZUM *is not used to being spoken to in this fashion, and for a moment is lost for words*)

MRS SQUEEZUM (*moving towards Ramble*) You are very uncivil to my husband, sir.

RAMBLE. Oh, madam! I beg your pardon. I did not know with whom I had the honour to be in company. It was always against my inclinations to affront a lady, and I trust I stand already acquitted in your opinion.

MRS SQUEEZUM (*won over already*) I hope, sir, it will only turn out to have been a frolic. I must own I have always been a great enemy to force—since there are so many willing.

RAMBLE (*aside*) So? I find there is little danger of a rape here.

MRS SQUEEZUM (*turning to her husband*) Well, honey, can you find anything against this gentleman?

SQUEEZUM. The woman is reluctant to confess in public, but I fancy when I examine her in private I may get it out of her. So, Mr Constable, withdraw your prisoner.

MRS SQUEEZUM (*hastily, for she is quite taken with Ramble*) Nay! Nay, he appears so much of a gentleman, that till there be stronger evidence, I will take charge of him. (*To Ramble*) Come, sir, you may drink a dish of tea with me. (*She turns to Staff*) You may stay without. (*She moves towards the steps leading to her boudoir*)

(STAFF *looks enquiringly at* SQUEEZUM, *but the Justice knows when he is beaten.* SQUEEZUM *signals for Staff to obey Mrs Squeezum, and* STAFF *turns and exits.* RAMBLE, *hardly able to believe his luck, hesitates a moment*)

(*Turning back*) Come, sir!

(RAMBLE *follows Mrs Squeezum, and they exit to her boudoir*)

SQUEEZUM (*all beguiling smiles, and climbing down from his desk*) Now, my child, you must realize it is better that ten innocent people should suffer than one guilty should escape.

HILARET. You may spare yourself further trouble, sir, for I assure you I will swear nothing.

SQUEEZUM. I see where your modesty lies. (*He moves closer to her*) You are afraid of spoiling your trade! Now tell me, how long have you been on the town?

HILARET. What do you mean, sir?

SQUEEZUM. Come, come! I see you are but a novice, and I like you the better for it. (*Going to embrace her*) Give us a kiss, eh?

(HILARET *escapes the old man's clutches with little difficulty. Meanwhile,* RAMBLE *and* MRS SQUEEZUM *have arrived in the boudoir, and the lights come up on Area 4*)

MRS SQUEEZUM. You will think I have a great deal of charity, who am not only the solicitor of your liberty with my husband, but can carry my good nature so far as to trust myself alone with you.

RAMBLE. I am deeply obliged to you, madam.

(*Down below,* SQUEEZUM *pauses in his chase to catch his breath*)

SQUEEZUM. Nay, be not coy with me. I protest you are as full of heart as a rose is of sweetness, and I as full of love as its stem of briars. If I thought you would prove constant, I would take you into keeping, for I have not liked a woman so much these many years.

HILARET (*aside, and a little amused in spite of herself*) I see I must humour this old devil a little.

(*In the boudoir* MRS SQUEEZUM *continues to ingratiate herself with* RAMBLE, *who plays his part gallantly*)

MRS SQUEEZUM. Wherefore do you imagine I ventured myself alone with you?

RAMBLE. From your great humanity, madam.

MRS SQUEEZUM. Alas, sir! It was to try whether you were really the man you were reported to be.

(*Below,* HILARET *has decided to brave the situation out*)

SQUEEZUM. What think you, my dear? Could you prove constant to a vigorous, healthy, middle-aged man, hey? (*He produces a purse from his pocket*) Come, take this purse as an earnest of what I'll do for you.

HILARET. What am I to do for this?

SQUEEZUM. Do? You shall do nothing. *I* will do. I will be the verb active and you shall be the verb passive. Do you follow my grammar, you little rogue?

HILARET. A little, sir! I trust you be not of the neuter gender. My father was a country parson and he gave all his children a good education.

SQUEEZUM. All his children? Tell me, my dear, do you have sisters?

HILARET. Alack-a-day, sir, sixteen of us. And all in the same way of business.

SQUEEZUM (*shaking his head sadly*) That's what comes of teaching daughters to read and write.

(*In the boudoir* Mrs SQUEEZUM *is finding* RAMBLE *a willing victim of her blandishments*)

MRS SQUEEZUM. And I am certain I find you as inoffensive, quiet, civil, well-bred a gentleman as any virtuous woman could wish. For your behaviour is so modest I could never imagine it possible you could have been guilty of what you are charged withal.

(*Below,* HILARET *is desperately improvising a whole new life-history for herself*)

SQUEEZUM. Sure the spirit of love must run strong in your whole family.

HILARET. Oh, sir, it was the crew of a battleship that put into harbour near us. My poor sisters were ruined by the officers, and I —fell a victim to their chaplain. (*She weeps*)

(*Up above,* MRS SQUEEZUM *is happily in* RAMBLE's *arms*)

MRS SQUEEZUM. Nay, I should be happy to trust myself any-where with so modest a gentleman.

RAMBLE. I'll take care, madam, not to forfeit your good opinion of me, for I swear by this soft hand, these lips, and all the million charms that dwell in this dear body, you can trust yourself with me anywhere.

(*In the Justice's room,* SQUEEZUM *is comforting* HILARET, *and taking her a little closer to his desk*)

SQUEEZUM. Come, come, my dear, you must dry your eyes. Though we have not all the conveniences of a battleship, yet you will find we are not altogether unprepared. (*He operates a catch at the top of the desk, and the front face folds down forming a divan. With a dexterity that can only result from much practice, he leads his latest victim to her doom*)

HILARET. Be not so hot, sir.

SQUEEZUM (*ardently*) You might as well bid the touchwood be cold beneath the burning glass . . .

(*Above,* MRS SQUEEZUM *is in a flutter of delighted anticipation*)

MRS SQUEEZUM. Nay, I protest and vow . . . Nay, sir.

RAMBLE. Protestations are as vain as struggling. (*He releases her a moment and looks round the boudoir*) Surely your closet has a bed in it.

(*Displaying an agility equal to her husband's,* MRS SQUEEZUM *operates a catch on the wall above the seat, and the bed drops down on its hinges. As it lands it makes a slight bump, which gives pause to the activity below)*

SQUEEZUM (*looking up in alarm*) But, hark, I hear my wife returning.

(*In the boudoir,* RAMBLE *is leading Mrs Squeezum towards the bed*)

MRS SQUEEZUM. Sir, sir, I beg you, no!

(*Below,* SQUEEZUM *hastily leaves Hilaret alone, and moves to the foot of the steps*)

SQUEEZUM (*calling up*) Honey, how are you doing up there? Have you nearly finished?

MRS SQUEEZUM (*pitching her voice in an unconcerned manner*) I'll be done in less than two minutes, my sweet.

SQUEEZUM (*calling again, suspiciously, and moving a step towards the boudoir*) My love!

MRS SQUEEZUM (*calling back, as calmly as she can manage*) Coming! (*Alarmed, to Ramble*) What shall I do?

RAMBLE (*not wishing to be interrupted*) Love shall instruct thee. Come!

SQUEEZUM (*moving another step, calling*) My love!

MRS SQUEEZUM (*answering him*) Coming! (*To Ramble*) No! Some other time. I dare not run any risk here.

RAMBLE (*still zealous*) I will not part with you.

SQUEEZUM (*another step*) My love!

MRS SQUEEZUM (*losing her temper, calling back*) Coming! (*To Ramble*) You shall hear from me. You shall have your liberty.

RAMBLE. With you?

MRS SQUEEZUM (*hastily escorting him to the boudoir door*) Yes, with me as well.

(MRS SQUEEZUM *hastily tidies herself and prepares to join her husband below.* SQUEEZUM, *assured of the imminence of his wife's arrival, hurries back to Hilaret. He folds up the divan and fastens it away*)

SQUEEZUM (*in a conspirator's whisper*) We must meet later at the *Eagle Tavern*. I will send a letter appointing you where to meet me. Enquire for "Mr Jones".

HILARET (*entering into the spirit*) "Mr Jones".

SQUEEZUM. My little honeysuckle.

HILARET. Bumble bee!

(HILARET *takes her leave and exits.* MRS SQUEEZUM *comes down the steps and moves to* SQUEEZUM, *who is now all innocent smiles.* RAMBLE *slowly follows Mrs Squeezum down*)

Mrs Squeezum. Well, honey, is the lady determined to swear?

Squeezum. Truly it is hard to say what she determines. She's gone to ask the advice of a divine, and a lawyer.

(Staff *enters*)

Mrs Squeezum (*offhand, and indicating Ramble*) I swear I can make nothing of that fellow.

Squeezum. I have a mind to discharge him.

Mrs Squeezum (*in sudden panic*) Nay! (*Recovering herself*) Nay, nay For I'm sure he hath money.

(Staff *lays a hand on Ramble's shoulder, and* Ramble *realizes he is still under arrest*)

Squeezum. What if he will not part with it?

Mrs Squeezum. Try him a little longer. I'll pay him a visit at the constable's house and try if I can frighten him. I may make him do more than you imagine.

Squeezum. Do so, my dear. I doubt not your power. (*He begins to move off*)

Mrs Squeezum. And pray don't forget my hundred guineas, honey.

Squeezum (*turning and forcing a smile*) I shan't forget them, Honey. Mr Constable, look to the prisoner. See him safely bestowed at your house. (*He exits*)

(Staff *exits, taking the reluctant* Ramble *with him*)

WHEN DOES THE RAVISHING BEGIN?   No. 7

Mrs Squeezum (*singing, plaintively*)
Patience is a virtue
Very few possess
And I confess
I feel myself
Possess it less and less;
But then, if you've
Already lost one virtue,
How on earth can
Losing one more hurt you?

(*With joyful abandon*) When Does the Ravishing Begin?
You could burst me with a pin
So much sin I'm holding in!
Men, come and catch a sitting hen
Who is contemplating When
Does the Ravishing Begin?

Lor!
Must I wait

In this state
For the pretty fellow
Or
Illustrate
What they made
Him a pretty fellow
For?
I've a mind
To incline
To the pretty fellow
More and more! Oh—

When Does the Ravishing Begin?
Tho' my smile is coy and win-
—some, it's fixing in a grin.
I'm in his grip, but he
Will not take a liberty!
Oh, when Does the Ravishing Begin?

(*In the orchestra a high, bird-like call is played*)

(*Imitating the phrase*) Ah-ah-ah-ah,
                   Ah-ah-ah-ah!

(*Another call from the orchestra, ending higher*)

(*In imitation*)   Ah-ah-ah-ah,
                   Ah-ah-ah-ah!

(*The orchestra again, still higher*)

(*In imitation*)   Ah-ah-ah-ah,
                   Ah-ah-ah-ah!

(*A final phrase from the orchestra, right out of reach*)
(*She makes as if to repeat this one, but decides with a shrug not to attempt the impossible*)

When Does the Ravishing Begin?
For I really have no doubt
That I'm going to try him out.
Him I shall try to capture
Think of the joy and rapture
When Does the Ravishing Begin?

Eeek!
I shall swoon
Very soon
For the fellow has me
Weak
At the thought
Of the sport,
And the fellow has me
Meek

And as mild
As a child
Till the fellow has me
Cheek to cheek! Oh—

When Does the Ravishing Begin?
Though he thinks I won't give in
I'm prepared to let him win.
I can't afford to dally
Why all this shilly-shally
When Does the Ravishing Begin?

(*During the applause, under cover of darkness,* Mrs Squeezum *exits,* Politic *and* Justice Worthy· *take their seats in Politic's parlour*)

Politic. I am distracted, utterly distracted. My daughter has vanished into thin air.

Worthy. But do you know of no reason for her flight?

Politic. There hath been a fellow in a red coat with whom she has conversed for some time, in spite of me.

Worthy. Depend on it, he is the occasion of your loss.

Politic. Why should scarlet hold such charms in the eyes of a woman? The Roman senate kept their armies abroad to prevent their sharing in their lands at home; and we should do the same to prevent their sharing our wives. A tall lusty fellow can make more work for a midwife in one winter at home than he can for a surgeon in ten summers abroad!

Worthy. I can grant you a warrant against him, if you know his name, though I fear you are too late. I should advise you to follow the example of the emperor who, when he discovered something worse than a marriage between his daughter and one of his subjects . . .

Politic. Pray, sir, what emperor was that?

Worthy. I think it was one of the Turks.

Politic. Bring me no example from the Turks, Justice Worthy. I dread and abhor the Turks.

Worthy. But, sir . . .

Politic (*interrupting*) But me no buts! What can be the reason of all this warlike preparation, which our newspapers have informed us of?

(*As the scene proceeds, Hilaret's lover,* Constant, *takes his place in the central Area 5, which now becomes the prison cell in Staff's house*)

Worthy. But what has all this to do with your daughter?

Politic. Never tell me of my daughter, sir. My country means more to me than a thousand daughters. Should the Turks come amongst us, what would become of our daughters then? And our sons, and our wives, and our estates, and our houses, and our religion, and our liberty? Give me leave, sir, only to let you a little into the present danger.

WORTHY (*rising*) I must beg to be excused, sir. If I can be of any service to you, in relation to your daughter, you have only to command me. I may perhaps defend you from your own countrymen, but truly from the Turks I cannot.

(CLORIS *enters and climbs up to Hilaret's bedroom, hardly daring to hope that her mistress has escaped unhurt from the scuffle in which they were parted*)

POLITIC. Perhaps you are not sufficiently appraised of the danger. Pray give me leave only to show you how they might easily make an inroad into Europe.

WORTHY (*moving away to* C) Dear sir, keep it 'til some other time. You have sufficiently satisfied me, I assure you. (*Bowing*) Mr Politic, your very humble servant.

POLITIC. And I, Justice Worthy, I am your most humble and obedient servant. (*He mumbles to himself ill-temperedly, as Worthy takes his leave*) What is the honour of my daughter compared with the news of the world?

WORTHY (*pausing* L *of* C) What an enthusiasm must his political studies have reached when they can make him forget the loss of his only daughter! But the greatest part of mankind labour under one kind of lunacy or another. The Coffee-House Politician, the covetous, the prodigal, the superstitious, the libertine, the lover. All are lunatics in their several ways.

(WORTHY *exits* L *as* HILARET *hurries on, up stage, and climbs the back steps to her bedroom*)

HILARET. Dear Cloris!

CLORIS. Dear madam, is it you? (*They embrace*) And are you intact?

HILARET. Intact? Oh, yes, thank heaven! I was like to have lost something, but all's safe I assure you.

CLORIS. Ah, I wish it were.

HILARET. What? Don't you believe me?

CLORIS. I wish you could not believe me, or I myself. Poor Captain Constant!

HILARET. What of him?

CLORIS. Oh, madam!

HILARET. Speak quickly, or kill me.

CLORIS. He's taken up for rape.

HILARET. Nay, impossible! I could never entertain such a belief against a man who hath given me such proofs of his constancy; besides, an affair of my own makes me the more doubtful of the truth of this. But if there appear any proof of such a fact, I will drive him for ever from my thoughts.

CLORIS. Oh, but he's quite innocent, madam. It was in an attempt to protect me from a ruffian's attack that he was arrested. (*Grimly*) But Justice Squeezum will take care to furnish the proof.

HILARET (*brightening at once*) Justice Squeezum! *That* rogue of a Justice? Oh, I could hug you for that! Let us not lose a moment. We must fly!

CLORIS. But, madam, will you venture forth again, and the hour so late?

HILARET. For Captain Constant I will venture anything. I'll watch outside his cell tonight, and tomorrow, come what may, I'll find some way to gain admittance.

CLORIS. But, madam . . .

HILARET. We will contrive something, never fear. And for tonight, at least I will be near him.

(*Despairing of ever putting sense into a head full of young love,* CLORIS *exits. A spotlight reveals* CAPTAIN CONSTANT *in his prison cell,* C)

LOVELY LOVER   No. 8

HILARET (*singing; in her bedroom, but very close to Constant in spirit*)
    Lovely lover,
    Fa-la-la-la,

CONSTANT (*dreaming of Hilaret, in his prison cell; singing*)
    Fa-la-la-la,

HILARET.   Fa-la-la-la,

CONSTANT.   Lovely lover,
    Fa-la-la-la,

HILARET.   These are the things you are.

CONSTANT.   La-la, . . .

HILARET.   . . . Fa-la-la,

CONSTANT.   Lovely lover,
    Heigh lack-a-day

HILARET.   Heigh lack-a-day,

CONSTANT.   Heigh lack-a-day,

HILARET.   Lovely lover,
    Heigh lack-a-day,

CONSTANT.   Don't ever go away

HILARET.   Lover . . .

CONSTANT.   . . . stay, lover.

BOTH (*together*)   Where do
    The words to
    Describe you
    Exist?

CONSTANT.	For the only phrase inside
	My foolish head is this;
HILARET.	Oh, my honey,
	Oh, my love . . .
CONSTANT.	Lovely lover,
	Fa-la-la-la,
HILARET.	Fa-la-la-la,
CONSTANT.	Fa-la-la-la,
BOTH (*together*)	Lovely lover
	Fa-la-la-la,
	These are the things you are.
	Fa-la-la-la,
	La-la-la.

(*Under cover of darkness* HILARET *exits*)

CONSTANT. What a comical turn of fate has brought me here. I defend an unknown woman in the street, and witness my reward! That such a service should go unrequited is not remarkable, but, sure, to swear a rape against me for having rescued her from a ravisher is an unparalleled piece of ingratitude.

(STAFF *enters*)

STAFF. Captain, your servant. I suppose you will be glad of company? Here is a very civil gentleman, I assure you.

CONSTANT (*morosely*) I had rather be left alone.

STAFF. I have but this one prison room, Captain. Besides, I assure you, this is no common fellow but a very fine gentleman.

CONSTANT. What is the cause of his misfortune?

STAFF. A rape, Captain. No dishonourable offence. I wouldn't have brought any scoundrels into your honour's company. But this is an honest brother ravisher. I have ravished women myself formerly, but a wife blunts a man's edge.

(RAMBLE *enters*)

This way, Admiral.

CONSTANT (*jumping to his feet*) Ramble!

RAMBLE (*crossing quickly to Constant*) My dear Captain Constant! (*They shake hands warmly*)

CONSTANT. What in the name of wonder hath brought you to England?

RAMBLE. What in the devil's name brings you to the constable's, sir?

CONSTANT (*echoing Staff*) Nothing dishonourable . . . only a rape.

RAMBLE. You jest.

STAFF. No, sir, upon my word. The captain is in earnest.

RAMBLE. Well, give me thy hand, brother, for our fortunes agree exactly.

STAFF. Allow me to congratulate you both. Whatever my house affords is at your service.

(STAFF *exits*)

RAMBLE. But tell me, Captain, I hope you have not really committed a rape. (*He sits*)

CONSTANT. I rescued a woman in the street, for which she was kind enough to swear a rape against me. But it gives me no uneasiness equal to the pleasure I enjoy at seeing you again. (*He sits*)

RAMBLE. And I in you, good Captain!

CONSTANT. But pray, how came you to leave the Indies, where I thought you had settled for life?

RAMBLE. Why, for the same reason that I went thither, that I am now here, by which I live, and for which I live.

CONSTANT. A woman?

RAMBLE. Right. A fine young rich woman! With four-score thousand pounds in her pocket!

CONSTANT. And what is her name?

RAMBLE. Her name is Ramble.

CONSTANT. What! Married?

RAMBLE. Ay. Soon after you left the Indies.

CONSTANT. I wish you joy, dear Jack. This thy good fortune fills me with delight.

RAMBLE. But I have not unfolded half yet . . .

(*He is about to continue with his story when* SOTMORE'S *voice is heard off stage.* CONSTANT *and* RAMBLE *react at once*)

SOTMORE (*off*) Let two quarts of rum be made into punch. And let it be hot!

CONSTANT. Good grief! Sotmore!

(SOTMORE *enters, followed by* STAFF. SOTMORE *is not under arrest, and* STAFF *holds no fears for him. Drunk or sober he has a natural air of authority when dealing with such menials*)

SOTMORE (*surprised to find Constant there*) Captain! Ho ho! (*He turns to Ramble*) So! Mark Anthony made a fine bargain, did he, when he gave the world for a woman?

RAMBLE. Hearkee, Sotmore, if you say anything against the ladies we'll cut your throat, and toss in a murder into the bargain.

SOTMORE. Not speak against women! You shall as soon compel me not to drink—and to do that you'll have to sew up my mouth. (*He turns to Staff*) Here, you, let the punch be gotten ready.

STAFF. It shall, an't please your honour.

(STAFF *exits*)

CONSTANT. You must not rail against the ladies, Sotmore, before Ramble, for he is a married man.

RAMBLE. And, what is more, my wife is at the bottom of the sea.

SOTMORE. And, what is worse, all her effects are at the bottom of the sea with her. I would not ensure a ship that had a woman on board for double the price. The sins of a woman are enough to draw down a judgement on a whole fleet.

CONSTANT. How was she lost?

RAMBLE. A storm, and my ill stars. I took her to dine with the captain of one of our convoy, and had no sooner left her when a sudden violent storm arising, I lost sight of her ship, and from that day have never seen or heard of her.

SOTMORE. Nor ever will again, I heartily hope. Tho' as for her coffers, those I wish delivered out of the deep. But the sea knows its own good, and it will surely keep the money, though possibly it may refund him the woman. (*He turns on Ramble with assumed severity*) But all this is a judgement on thee for breaking thy word! Did I not tell thee thou wert strolling off to some beastly little wench?

RAMBLE. But, honest Nol, how didst thou find me out?

SOTMORE. Find you out! Why the whole town rings of you! There is not a husband or guardian in it but what is ready to get drunk for joy that you're under lock and key. You are a nuisance, sir! (*He rises and moves to Constant*) I don't believe he hath been in town six days, and he's already had about sixteen women.

RAMBLE (*jumping up and joining them*) Seventeen!

(*The three friends laugh, join arms, and—as the music begins—go into a gay and abandoned dance*)

LOCK UP YOUR DAUGHTERS   No. 9

SOTMORE (*breaking free and singing*)
        Lock Up Your Daughters
        Here comes a rake!
        Lock Up Your Daughters
        Their chastity's at stake.
        Here is a man with one
            Thought in his head;
      "Whom can I court, and
          Escort into bed?"
        Go round and knock up the
        Locksmith to Lock Up
        Your Daughters now!

(SOTMORE *rejoins Ramble as* CONSTANT *steps forward*)

CONSTANT (*singing*)
>Lock Up Your Daughters
>Spring's in the air.
>Lock Up Your Daughters
>For wedding rings are rare.
>You'd be amazed at the
>>Things they can delve
>Into if they are not
>>In before twelve!
>Wind ev'ry clock up and
>You'd better Lock Up
>Your Daughters now!

(*The three link arms again and resume their dance as they sing together*)

ALL (*together*)
>Lock Up Your Daughters
>Safely at home.
>Lock Up Your Daughters
>Where fancy cannot roam.

RAMBLE (*singing*)
>Out on the streets there are
>>Others like me
>Looking for possible
>>Mothers-to-be
>Building a stock up, so

ALL (*together*)
>You'd better Lock Up
>Your Daughters now!

(*The orchestra plays another chorus as the boys continue their dance*)

ALL (*together, with increasing urgency*)
>Lock Up Your Daughters!
>They're all the same.
>Lock Up Your Daughters
>Before they come to shame.
>Whether your daughter is
>>Pretty or plain.
>Once she has done it, she'll
>>Do it again.
>Fathers!
>Lock Up Your Daughters
>Now!

(*They end their dance and return, happily breathless, to their seats by the table. At that moment* HILARET *enters*)

HILARET (*ignoring Ramble and hurrying to her lover*) My Constant!

CONSTANT (*taking her in his arms*) My Hilaret!

RAMBLE (*recognizing Hilaret and moving hastily out of her line of vision*) Heyday! What, are we both in for the same woman? (*He observes their rapturous greeting*) I suspect by her fondness he's already ravished her.

CONSTANT. Oh, Hilaret! This kindness of yours sinks me the deeper. Can you bear to think of one accused of such a crime as I am?

(CONSTANT *and* HILARET *continue a mimed conversation*)

RAMBLE (*aside*) Hey! The devil! Is this Constant's mistress?

SOTMORE (*moving to Ramble*) Is this the lady that did you the favour?

RAMBLE (*pretending hardly to recognize her*) This the lady? No! This is a woman of virtue, though she has a great resemblance to the other, I must confess.

HILARET (*to Constant*) You were in the same scuffle which parted me and my maid in Leicester Fields?

CONSTANT. Yes, I was there. And the adventure befell me while I was on my way to our appointment.

HILARET. You rescued my maid from an assault, while I was being assaulted elsewhere.

(HILARET *turns to* RAMBLE, *who flinches slightly in preparation for the supposed forthcoming revelation*)

Which, that I escaped, I have to thank this gentleman.

RAMBLE (*barely able to believe his luck*) Oh, madam! Your most obedient, humble servant. Was it you, dear lady?

CONSTANT. Is it possible my friend can have so far indebted me? This is a favour I can never return!

RAMBLE. You overrate it, upon my soul you do.

CONSTANT (*warmly*) I can never repay thee. Hadst thou given me the world, it could not have equalled the least favour conferred on this lady.

RAMBLE (*aside*) I should have conferred some favours on her indeed, if she would have let me!

CONSTANT. My dear Ramble, tell me the whole story.

RAMBLE (*deciding he had better make it a good one*) I had no sooner parted from (*indicating Sotmore*) this gentleman, when I heard a young lady's voice crying out for help. I think the word rape was mentioned, but that I cannot perfectly remember. Thereupon, making directly to the place where the noise proceeded, I found this lady in the arms of a very rude fellow . . .

HILARET (*admiring his nerve and secretly amused; supporting his story*) The most impudent fellow, sure, that ever was born!

RAMBLE. A very impudent fellow, and yet a very cowardly one. For, the moment I came up, he quitted his hold and was gone in the twinkling of an eye.

Constant (*overflowing with gratitude*) My dear Ramble! What hast thou done for me?

Ramble. I would have done the same for any man breathing.

Constant. I pray that heaven may send me an opportunity of serving thee in the same manner!

(Ramble *acknowledges the magnanimity behind this generous offer, then turns aside*)

Ramble (*to himself*) May that be the only prayer which it denies thee!

(Staff *enters*)

Staff. The punch is ready, gentlemen. You may walk down. The liberty of my house is at your service.

(Sotmore *receives this news with enthusiasm, takes* Ramble *by the arm and they exit.* Staff *follows them, and for a moment* Hilaret *and* Constant *are alone. They seize the opportunity to kiss, as lovers will, and the music begins. As they slowly follow their friends, they sing a reprise of their duet, as Finale to Act I*)

LOVELY LOVER (*Reprise*)   No. 10

Hilaret (*singing, with tender feeling*)	Lovely lover,
	Fa-la-la-la,
Constant (*singing*)	Fa-la-la-la,
Hilaret.	Fa-la-la-la,
Constant.	Lovely lover,
	Fa-la-la-la,
Hilaret.	These are the things you are.
Constant.	La-la . . .
Hilaret.	. . . Fa-la-la.
Constant.	Lovely lover,
	Heigh lack-a-day,
Hilaret.	Heigh lack-a-day,
Constant.	Heigh lack-a-day,
Hilaret.	Lovely lover,
	Heigh lack-a-day,
Constant.	Don't ever go away.
Hilaret.	Lover . . .
Constant.	. . . Stay, lover.

BOTH (*together*)	Where do
	The words to
	Describe you
	Exist?
HILARET.	For the only phrase inside
	My foolish head is this
CONSTANT.	Tell me, honey,
	Tell me.
HILARET.	Lovely lover,
	Fa-la-la-la,
CONSTANT.	Fa-la-la-la,
HILARET.	Fa-la-la-la,
BOTH (*together*)	Lovely lover,
	Fa-la-la-la,
	These are the things you are.
	Fa-la-la-la,
	Fa-la-la.

ACT II

When Act II begins, the Area of Justice Squeezum's room is lit. The lugubrious QUILL *is standing by the Justice's desk, studying it with the baleful contempt he privately reserves for his employer. A mischievous thought lights his face for an instant, and he assumes the Squeezum stance and expression, and climbs on to the stool behind the desk. For a few moments he tastes the fruits of power—dealing severely with an imaginary offender, accepting bribes with surreptitious condescension, and—with relish—rapping the desk with his gavel to call an impertinent prisoner—or his inattentive clerk to order. Chuckling to himself, he turns with a typical Squeezum-type gesture and freezes in horror as he finds himself staring into the face of* JUSTICE SQUEEZUM *in person, who has entered quietly and watched the last few seconds of this performance)*

SQUEEZUM. Do not anticipate such rapid advancement, Quill.

(With a sickly smile of near-apology QUILL *climbs down from the desk, his brief reign of terror over)*

You reserved me a private room at the *Eagle Tavern*?

QUILL *(anxious to be back in favour)* Yes, sir, yes. Shall I attend you to the tavern tonight?

SQUEEZUM *(with almost a smile)* Not tonight, Quill. I shall be travelling incognito. I have—*(airily)* a mission of some delicacy to attend to.

QUILL. I think I understand, sir.

SQUEEZUM *(afraid that this is only too true)* Yes, Quill. You have ever a sharp understanding. So much so that I think I may trust you with a secret. And what I am going to tell you will show you what a confidence I put in you. In short, Quill, I suspect my wife.

QUILL. Of what, sir?

SQUEEZUM. I fear I am not the only person free with her.

*(QUILL *receives the news with exaggerated surprise. This has been the best-known secret in town; but the husband is always the last to know)*

Therefore, Quill, as it is in your power to observe her, I assure you a very handsome reward on her conviction. *(He turns away a little)* For if I do not discover her, I fear she will shortly discover me.

QUILL. Sir, I shall be as diligent as possible.

SQUEEZUM. And I as liberal, upon your success. *(He exits)*

QUILL (*grumbling to himself, as usual*) I know him and his liberality. My mistress will reward services better than he will. Besides, I have too much honour to take fees on both sides. I'll go, like an honest and dutiful servant, and tell my mistress of this conspiracy. (*He starts in the direction of Mrs Squeezum's boudoir, but pauses and turns back for a moment to give a sharp, rhythmic whisper which sets the Cha-Cha beat for the next musical number*) There's a Plot A-foot! (*He continues another step or two towards the boudoir*)

THERE'S A PLOT AFOOT   No. 12

(*He turns and whispers again*)

There's a Plot A-Foot!

(JUSTICE SQUEEZUM *enters, cloaked in mystery*)

SQUEEZUM (*singing*)   There's a Plot A-Foot,
                        Ha! Ha! Ha!
                        Which involves a little lady
                        And a shady
                        Local Inn.

                        There's a Plot A-Foot
                        Ha! Ha! Ha!
                        Where the little lady wavers
                        And her favours
                        I will win.

(*The stage begins to fill with all the sinister figures involved in "the plot". HILARET arrives from her bedroom*)

HILARET (*singing*)   He thinks
                        That we think
                        There's nothing to be done.
                        He'll go
                        And I'll go,
                        And when he thinks he's won,
                        You'll find
                        That he'll find
                        That two can have their fun
                        He's got a plot
EVERYONE (*singing*)   But we've got a plot

(*From Politic's parlour, POLITIC and DABBLE, conspirators at international level, join the others*)

POLITIC and DABBLE (*singing together*)
                        There's a Plot A-Foot,
                        Ha! Ha! Ha!

To reform Constantinople
Or the Pope'll
Sack Beirut.

There's a Plot A-Foot
Ha! Ha! Ha!
Yes, it's murmured in the city
There's a pretty
Plot a-foot.

(FAITHFUL *stumbles on from Politic's house. At his age things do not sink in as quickly as they did—but he has his suspicions*)

FAITHFUL (*spoken*) I think there's a plot a-foot! Someone's tampered with my young mistress!

(MRS SQUEEZUM, *most ardent plotter of them all, descends from her boudoir*)

MRS SQUEEZUM (*singing*)

There's a Plot A-Foot,
Ha! Ha! Ha!
To release a certain party
Who's a hearty
Young upstart.

There's a Plot A-Foot
Ha! Ha! Ha!
To invite him to my closet
And deposit
All my heart.

(*The* WHOLE COMPANY *dances—the routine having the style and shape of a Minuet, but the rhythm of a Cha-Cha*)

MEN	WOMEN
(*singing together*)	
There's a	
plot afoot! Ha! Ha! Ha!	He thinks that we think
Which involves a little lady	There's nothing to be done
And a shady	He'll go and I'll go
local inn.	And when he thinks he's won
Plot afoot!	You'll find that he'll find
Plot afoot!	That two can have their fun.

SQUEEZUM (*singing, still gleeful*)
I've got a plot!

EVERYONE ELSE (*singing together*)
> But we've got a plot!

(SOTMORE *joins the conspirators. As the number moves to a conclusion,* CONSTANT *and* RAMBLE *resume their places in the cell of Staff's house, in Area 5*)

SOTMORE (*singing*)   There's a Plot A-Foot,
> Ha! Ha! Ha!
> You can bet a pint of swill on
> Where the villain
> Will be put.
>
> There's a Plot A-Foot,
> Ha! Ha! Ha!
> Yes, it's murmured in the city
> There's a pretty
> Plot a-foot.

SQUEEZUM (*spoken*)   Ha! Ha! Ha!
POLITIC and DABBLE (*spoken together*)
> Ha! Ha! Ha!
EVERYONE (*spoken together*)
> Ha! Ha! Ha!

(*Under cover of darkness, all exit except* CONSTANT, RAMBLE *and* SOTMORE. *When the lights come up on Area 5, they are discovered in "the cell".*
> STAFF *enters*)

STAFF. You are both requested to await Justice Squeezum's pleasure here. Your cases will be heard this morning. Since the charges are identical Justice Squeezum reckons he can hear both at the same time, and so save expenses. Wait, and I will go fetch him.

(STAFF *exits*)

CONSTANT (*to Ramble*) Since Hilaret will not appear against you, and her maid will not appear against me, on what evidence does he hope to convict us?

RAMBLE. Be assured this rogue of a justice has no need of evidence. But comfort yourself with the expectation of revenge, for I think he cannot possibly escape the net we have spread.

CONSTANT. Well, let us hope for the best. (*He moves closer to Ramble*) But what do you intend in England, where you have no friends?

RAMBLE. I know not yet whether I have or not. I left an ageing father here who saw fit to turn me out of doors for some frolics. It is probable, if he yet lives, he may have forgiven me by this. But what's become of him I know not, for I have not heard one word of him these ten years.

(STAFF *returns*)

STAFF. The Justice has been called out on urgent business. (*He crosses to Ramble*) Here's a letter for you, sir. From his wife. (*He hands a letter to Ramble, turns and leaves*)

RAMBLE (*opening the letter and reading it aloud*) "Sir, I was no sooner recovered from the fright you gave me than I have performed my promise. You will find me waiting in my room. The constable hath ordered to acquit you." (*Delightedly, he moves down stage*) Here's a good nature for you! Thou dear wife of a damn rogue of a justice—I fly to your arms.

CONSTANT (*following Ramble down*) But wait! Suppose you brought her to be a witness to our design. (*He takes a letter from his pocket*) Here, take this letter of assignation from Squeezum to Hilaret! (*He hands the letter to Ramble*) It will give your discovery credit.

(RAMBLE *begins his "journey" towards Mrs Squeezum's boudoir*)

(*Calling after him*) And success attend you!

(*When the lights dim out on the cell,* CONSTANT *and* SOTMORE *make their exit. Meanwhile, in her boudoir,* MRS SQUEEZUM *is making herself beautiful for her eagerly-awaited visitor*)

WHEN DOES THE RAVISHING BEGIN?   No. 13
(*Reprise*)

(RAMBLE *begins his climb up the steps to the boudoir in time with the first notes of the introduction*)

MRS SQUEEZUM (*singing*) When Does the Ravishing Begin?
                         You could burst me with a pin
                         So much sin I'm holding in!

RAMBLE (*singing*)   Men, watch me catch a sitting hen
                         Who is contemplating
                         When Does the Ravishing Begin?

MRS SQUEEZUM.   Eek!

BOTH (*together*)   I shall
                        She will swoon

                        Very soon

                        For the fellow has me
                                            her

                        Weak
                        At the thought
                        Of the sport

                        And the fellow has me
                                            her

	Meek And as mild As a child
Mrs Squeezum.	Till the fellow has me Cheek to cheek! Oh—
	When Does the Ravishing Begin?
Ramble.	Tho' her smile is coy and win- -some, it's fixing in a grin.
Mrs Squeezum.	I'm in his grip, but he Will not take a liberty! Oh, when?
Ramble (*getting nearer*)	Soon!
Mrs Squeezum.	When?
Ramble (*at the door of the boudoir*)	Soon!
Mrs Squeezum.	When Does the Ravishing Begin?
Ramble (*hastily moving to embrace her; shouting*)	Now!

(Mrs Squeezum *gives a delighted yelp and the lights on the boudoir black-out. After a short pause, lights come up on Politic's parlour, where* Politic *and* Dabble *are at their favourite occupation—wading through the day's issue of newsprint*)

Dabble. What think you of the *Daily Equivocator?*

Politic. I don't know. I have had no time to read it yet. I have only read (*checking quickly through the pile, and putting publications on one side as he names them*) the *London Journal*, the *County Journal*, the *Weekly Journal*, *Applebee's Journal*, the *British Journal*, the *British Gazette*, the *Morning Post*, the *Coffee-House Morning Post*, the *Daily Post-Boy*, the *Daily Journal*, the *Daily Courant*, the *Gazette*, the *Evening Post*, the *Whitehall Evening Post*, the *London Evening Post*, and the *St James's Evening Post*. (*He composes himself*) Pray, sir, read to me from the *Equivocator*.

Dabble. "Berlin, June tenth. We hear certain rumours here concerning certain measures taken by a certain northern potentate, but cannot certainly learn either who that potentate is, or what are the measures he hath taken. Meantime, we are assured with certainty, that time will bring them all to light."

Politic (*having pondered this a few seconds*) Pray, sir, read that last over again.

Dabble. "Meantime, we are assured with certainty, that time will bring them to light."

Politic (*very deeply*) Ah, yes. Yes!

DABBLE. I like these papers that disappoint you with good news! Where the beginning of a paragraph threatens you with war and the latter part ensures your peace.

POLITIC. Yes, yes. Read on, pray, read on.

DABBLE. "However, this is all guess-work, and till such time as we see an actual hostility committed, we must leave our readers in the same uncertain state we found them."

POLITIC. Hum! I find there is no certainty to be come at. It may be either peace or war.

DABBLE. Though were I to lay a wager, I should choose war. For, if you observe, we are twice assured of that, whereas we have only one affirmation on the side of peace. But stay, perhaps the next paragraph may decide the issue. "Fontainbleu, June fourteenth. It is observable that a certain ambassador hath for several days past been in close conference with the minister of a certain state, which causes various speculations. But as we know neither the said minister's name, nor his state, nor the matter in debate, we cannot yet say what may be the consequence thereof."

POLITIC (*looks as if he is about to produce a profound conclusion, then alters his mind*) Pray, sir, read that last over again.

DABBLE (*after a sigh*) "As we know neither the said minister's name, nor his state . . ."

(*In great agitation* FAITHFUL *and* CLORIS *enter and stand above Politic's table*)

FAITHFUL. Oh, sir, Cloris hath brought the strangest news of my young mistress.

POLITIC (*hardly looking up*) Do not interrupt us, blockhead!

FAITHFUL. If you lose a moment, she may be lost for ever!

POLITIC. Peace, sirrah, peace!

FAITHFUL. Sir, my young mistress will be undone, ruined, *hanged* if you do not assist her. She's been arrested. Oh! My poor young lady!

CLORIS. The sweetest, best-tempered lady that ever was born . . .

FAITHFUL (*losing his temper*) Can you sit there, sir, reading a parcel (*he picks a newspaper from the table*) of damned, confounded, lying nonsense, and not go to your own daughter's assistance? (*He waves the paper angrily in the air*)

POLITIC (*looking at him in astonishment*) Sure, the poor fellow is possessed!

FAITHFUL (*still brandishing the paper*) Sir, your daughter is possessed!

CLORIS. Possessed by constables!

FAITHFUL. She's been taken up for rape.

POLITIC. My daughter, taken up for rape? Sure something has touched the fellow's brain.

FAITHFUL. Ay, sir! And it would touch yours, too, if you had a grain of humanity in you. (*His eyes fall on an item in the paper he is holding*)

POLITIC. A woman taken up for rape? That's impossible! Even I know that.

FAITHFUL (*horrified*) But here it is! (*He thrusts the paper at Politic*) In this morning's paper!

(POLITIC *and* DABBLE *jump to their feet.* POLITIC *glances for an instant at the newspaper he is being shown, then nods helplessly at Dabble to confirm the truth of Faithful's story*)

IT MUST BE TRUE (*Reprise*)   No. 14

POLITIC, DABBLE, FAITHFUL and CLORIS (*singing together*)
> It must be true,
> For we read it in the papers, didn't you?
> It must be true,
> Very revolutionary point of view!
>
> And it's no use being
> An escapist, when
> All the papers say she's
> A rapist, then
>
> It must be true,
> Yet it's something that her
> Mother didn't . . .
> Something that her
> Mother didn't . . .
> Something that her
> Mother didn't do.

(FAITHFUL *produces his ear-trumpet, sounds the post-horn call on it, and they all chase off to the rescue.*

As the lighting changes, we see MRS SQUEEZUM *slinking seductively down the steps from her boudoir, a look of smug self-satisfaction on her face —the cat that stole the cream*)

THE GENTLE ART OF SEDUCTION   No. 14A

(*This additional number can be taken as a solo for* MRS SQUEEZUM, *or she can dance the number with* RAMBLE, *or she can be joined by the* FULL COMPANY *in Ensemble. Throughout,* MRS SQUEEZUM *uses stage-level, below Area 5, and her dance movements should be an exaggerated "apache-tango" in mood*)

MRS SQUEEZUM (*singing*)

The Gentle Art of Seduction,
The subtle art of seduction.
With a sigh he'll adore
You imply so much more
And paint such a picture in his brain.

The Gentle Art of Seduction
The crafty art of seduction
When he's hot for the spoil
Take the pot off the boil,
And then you can heat it up again!

Be daring, but never give way.
Be sparing, and watch what you say.
The fish is only baited—
But unsatiated.

Surrender leads to destruction
The Gentle Art of Seduction,
Isn't just what you do
Rather more what you don't.
Not just what you will,
Rather more what you won't.
Sing ri-fol-a-diddle-fol-de-lay.

The Gentle Art of Seduction,
That age-old art of seduction.
I perceive Adam's Eve
Knew what leaves she could leave
And still make the most of all her charms.

The Gentle Art of Seduction,
Delilah's art of seduction.
Though she practised for years
With a cracked pair of shears
Her Samson was happy in her arms.

Salome and Helen of Troy
May show me how well to employ
The gifts that I've been blessed with,
That I do my best with.

I'm open to misconstruction.
The Gentle Art of Seduction
Is the only device
That a female can use
She puts a price
On what she has to lose.

Sing ri-fol-a-diddle-fol-de-lay.

Let's end this course of instruction
The Gentle Art of Seduction
Is the fall of a sigh
When the girl murmurs "Oh"
The wink of an eye
When the girl murmurs "No"
Sing ri-fol-a-diddle
Fol-de-lay.

(*The stage empties under cover of darkness, and Area 5 becomes Brazen-court's Tavern again: an "upstairs room" in fact, but they probably look much alike. There should be a table and chair, a screen and mirror, some wine to drink and two glasses. If necessary, BRAZENCOURT and his SERVING WENCH can be setting the furniture and properties when the lights come up.*

    JUSTICE SQUEEZUM, gorgeously apparelled in the style of the young Bucks of the day, and inadequately disguised with a beauty spot on his cheek, enters and looks around eagerly)

SQUEEZUM. No woman been to enquire for Mr Jones?

BRAZENCOURT. Who?

SQUEEZUM (*confound the fellow's denseness*) Mr Jones!

BRAZENCOURT (*with a leer*) Oh, Mr Jones. (*He winks knowingly, then shakes his head*) No, Mr Squeezum. I know of none. (*He prepares to leave, taking the* WENCH *with him*) But I'll ask at the bar, if you please.

SQUEEZUM (*testy at having his disguise so easily penetrated*) Do. And leave word, if any such comes, to show her up at once.

BRAZENCOURT. Certainly, (*heavily*) Mr Jones.

(BRAZENCOURT *and the* WENCH *exit.* SQUEEZUM, *good humour restored, moves with sprightly step to the mirror to check his wig, run a finger over his eyebrows, give a last fillip to the lace of his cravat*)

MISTER JONES   No. 15

(*As the music begins,* SQUEEZUM *can no longer restrain his own feeling of ebullient well-being, and his spindly legs twinkle into a dance*)

SQUEEZUM (*singing*)   Just look at yourself!
            A picture of health!
            Such dashing agility—
            Full of virility—
            Sharp as a blade!
            No wonder the maid
            Is finding it hard to resist!

Mister Jones!
Do you recognize
  The feeling in your bones?
This familiar sensation—
Indescribable elation—
Can it mean rejuvenation,
Mister Jones?

Mister Jones
Is the man in full
  Control of what he owns?
Heaven knows, but Heaven rest it,
You will have a chance to test it
When the lady comes to call on
Mister Jones!

(*A few more dance steps, another appraising glance in the mirror*)

(*Spoken*) I protest this woman hath revived the full vigour of youth
in me! Sure, I must have over-reckoned my years! I cannot be
above . . . forty-five at the most!

(*Singing*)   You twiddle your thumbs
     'Til maybe she comes—
     Or maybe she doesn't
     Don't worry, you mustn't!
     Good heavens alive!
     She'll *have* to arrive,
     Or she'll never know what she's missed!

Mister Jones!
How your over-stuffed
  Imagination groans!
If you want to cut a dash on
Her, then this is not the fashion,
You will dissipate your passion,
Mister Jones!

Mister Jones!
Just to think they placed you
With the ancient crones!
There's a fortune in you, Lud!
If they could put you out to stud,
Until the lady comes to call on
Mister . . .

(*Pattering*)   Polish your buttons
     And tighten your rig.
(*Singing*)   The lady comes to call on
     Mister . . .

(Pattering)   Blow all the spider-webs
                       Out of your wig.

(Singing)   The lady comes to call on
                       Mister Jones!

> *(The old legs prove equal to another sprightly measure, but as the music ends he is grateful to sit down by the table and catch his breath.*
>
> *HILARET and SOTMORE arrive at the edge of the stage and hold a brief whispered consultation. SOTMORE wishes her "good luck" and exits. HILARET then approaches Squeezum)*

HILARET. Mr Jones?

SQUEEZUM (*jumping up at once and hastily disguising that he is rather short of breath*) Oh, there you are! You little, pretty, dear, sweet rogue! I have been waiting for you these four hours at least.

HILARET. Young lovers are commonly earlier than their appointments.

SQUEEZUM (*delighted*) Young lovers? Give me a kiss for that!

> *(HILARET has little option but to accept his peck on the cheek)*

Thou shalt find me a young lover, too. A vigorous young lover. (*He leads her to the table*) Come, sit down; sit down, and let me give you a glass of wine.

> *(They sit by the table and SQUEEZUM pours wine as he continues)*

Now, let me hear the story how you were first seduced, that I may set it down in my history at home. I have the history of all the women's ruin that ever I lay with. I call it "The History of My Own Times". I do. Truly I do! (*He passes a glass of wine to her*)

HILARET. I'll warrant it's as big as a church Bible!

SQUEEZUM. It really is a pretty good size. I have done execution in my time.

HILARET. And may do execution still!

SQUEEZUM. But now let me have the history: where did your amour begin? In a church, I warrant you. More amours begin in church than end there. Or perhaps you went to see the battleship you spoke of?

HILARET (*deciding this is as good a cue as any*) Ay, sir. It was there indeed that I first saw him. That was the fatal scene of our interview.

SQUEEZUM. And was the amour managed by letter or by word of mouth?

HILARET. By letter, sir.

SQUEEZUM. And how many letters did you write to him, eh? Before . . . well, before you . . . you know!

HILARET. Not many. He did not want much encouragement.

SQUEEZUM. Come to the last fatal meeting!

HILARET. It was a Sunday morning . . .

Squeezum (*almost crowing with delight*) Right! *My* old method exactly. When all the others are at church.

SUNNY SUNDAY MORNING   No. 16

(*The music begins and* Hilaret *moves down centre, eagerly watched by* Squeezum. *As the number proceeds,* Hilaret *performs a sedate strip-tease which has* Squeezum *in a frenzy of delight, although it consists of no more than the removal of her gloves, hat, and finally her gown. Since she is wearing underwear of the period, however, she appears to end up better covered than she was in the first place*)

Hilaret (*singing*) On a Sunny Sunday Morning
In the middle of the month of June
Fatigued with walking in the heat
I sought the shade of an arbour sweet,
For I felt that I was fit to swoon.

I found a place,
'Twas seeming fair,
But ah! disgrace!
A *man* was there!

Squeezum (*hugging himself; speaking*) The sly dog! My old way again. (*Urging her on*) And then . . . and then . . .

Hilaret.   On a Sunny Sunday Morning
In the middle of the month of June
He way-laid me so eagerly
Entreating me was I free to be
His beloved for the afternoon?

I asked the man
What *did* he mean?
And then began
That fatal scene.

Squeezum (*speaking*)
And then . . . and then?

Hilaret.   On a Sunny Sunday Morning
In the middle of the month of June
He flew at me and held me tight,
I fought him off with all my might,
But a lady weakens all too soon.

This fly at length
Was in his web;
I felt my strength
Begin to ebb.
He sighed—

SQUEEZUM (*sighing too*) Oh, my little honeysuckle . . .

HILARET.   I cried—

SQUEEZUM. Oh, my paradise . . .

HILARET.   He tried—

SQUEEZUM. Oh, my lovey-dove . . .

HILARET.   I died—
(*Spoken aside*)   —practically . . .
(*Singing*)   On a Sunny Sunday Morning.

(*As the music ends,* SQUEEZUM *closes on Hilaret and takes her hungrily into his arms*)

SQUEEZUM. Oh, I can endure it no longer.

HILARET (*with assumed astonishment, struggling*) What do you mean, sir?

SQUEEZUM. Mean? I mean to gobble you up—to swallow you down—to squeeze you all to pieces.

HILARET (*shouting off*) Help, there! A rape, a rape, a rape!

(SOTMORE *hurries on*)

SOTMORE. What in the devil's name's going on here? Justice Squeezum ravishing a woman!

(SQUEEZUM *releases Hilaret at the sound of Sotmore's voice.* HILARET *runs to Sotmore, begging protection*)

HILARET. Oh, for Heaven's sake, sir, assist a poor forlorn hapless maid whom this wicked man hath treacherously seduced.

SQUEEZUM. Oh, lud! Oh, lud! I am undone.

(*In the original presentation,* SQUEEZUM *now picked up Hilaret and carried her from the stage to the front row of the audience, and placed her on the most convenient male lap, then returning to the stage. The speeches in the following passage set in square brackets were addressed to the member of the audience concerned. In theatres where this piece of business is impracticable they can be omitted or adapted*)

SOTMORE. [You ought to be ashamed.] Fie upon you, Mr Squeezum. A magistrate, the preserver and executor of our laws, thus to be the breaker of them!

HILARET. For pity's sake, sir, secure him! Do not let him escape till we send for a constable.

SQUEEZUM. Oh, lud! What shame I have brought myself [and you too, sir.] That ever I should have lived to see this day!

SOTMORE. If thou hadst stuck to thy bottle like an honest fellow, this had never happened. But you must go a-whoring at your time of life. With those spindle shanks, that weazel face, that crane's neck of a body.

(HILARET *now takes leave of her new-found acquaintance and returns to the stage*)

Who would have imagined that such an old, withered maypole as him would attempt to fall on a woman? Why, thou wilt be the laughing-stock of the whole town!

Squeezum. Sir, if there be truth on earth, I am innocent.

Hilaret (*indicating Sotmore*) Was not this gentleman an eye-witness?

Sotmore. Ay, ay. I can swear to the rape with as safe a conscience as I can drink a glass of wine.

Squeezum. I see I am betrayed. I am caught in my own trap. (*Aside*) There is but one escape, which is the way I have opened to others. (*He turns to Hilaret with an air of defeat, ruefully accepted*) I see, madam, your design is to extort money from me. Well, I hope you will be reasonable, for I am very poor, I assure you. It is not for men of my honesty to be rich.

Hilaret (*haughtily*) Sir, if you gave me millions it would not satisfy my revenge!

Squeezum (*groaning, aside*) Here's a cruel wretch! She prefers my blood to my gold!

Sotmore (*crossing purposefully*) And now, sir, I'll go fetch a constable.

Squeezum (*hurrying to seize his arm*) Hold, hold, sir. For mercy's sake do not expose me so. (*Turning to Hilaret*) Will nothing content you, madam?

Hilaret. Nothing but the rigour of the law. (*Signalling to Sotmore*) Fetch the constable immediately.

Squeezum. I'll do anything. I'll consent to any terms.

Hilaret. The constable!

Squeezum (*now in a desperate panic*) I'll give you (*it almost chokes him*) a hundred guineas! I'll do anything!

Hilaret. Remember your vile commitment of two gentlemen this morning.

Squeezum. One is already released. The other shall be set free immediately.

Hilaret. Too late. (*She turns away*)

Sotmore. Harkye, sir. Will you leave off whoring and take to drinking for the future?

Squeezum. I will. Indeed, I will. I'll do anything, anything.

Sotmore. Then I'll intercede with this lady that, on your acquit-ting the gentleman, you shall be acquitted yourself.

Squeezum. I'll do anything, anything.

Sotmore (*crossing to Hilaret and giving a grand advocate's performance for Squeezum's benefit*) Madam, I beg you to be merciful to this poor, unfortunate and undutiful servant of justice.

Hilaret (*turning to him and melting*) Sir, I can deny you nothing.

Squeezum (*hurriedly, before she changes her mind again*) Get me a pen, ink and paper. I'll send an order to bring your friend hither, and release him immediately.

Sotmore (*calling off*) Bring pen, ink and paper, (*then a thought of his own*) and a bottle of old port.

Squeezum (*reproachfully, to Hilaret*) How could you have the conscience to swear against a poor old man?

Sotmore (*returning to them*) Faith, 'twas a little cruel. (*To Hilaret*) Could you have had the heart to see him languishing in his own gaol?

(Brazencourt *enters with paper, pen and ink, and a bottle of wine. He places them on the table*)

But here's the paper. Come, sir, write our friend's discharge. Constant's his name. Captain Constant. He must be set free immediately.

(Squeezum *does as he is told.* Brazencourt *exits*)

(*Setting a chair for Hilaret some distance from Squeezum*) You have managed this matter so well, you compel me to change my opinion of your sex.

Hilaret (*sitting*) Let a woman alone for a plot, Mr Sotmore.

Sotmore. Ay, madam, a woman that will drink. For wine is the fountain of ideas. Leave your damn'd tea-drinking and take to wine! It will paint your face better than vermilion, and put more honesty in your heart than all the sermons you can read. By all the pleasures of drinking, madam, you have made a conquest of me. If a bottle of burgundy were on one side, and you on the other, I don't know which I would choose. If we'd met earlier, I might have reformed you!

Hilaret (*with a smile*) Or I you, Mr Sotmore.

(Sotmore *shrugs sadly, admitting the possibility. The music begins*)

IF I'D KNOWN YOU   No. 17

Sotmore (*singing, almost as though in soliloquy*)
        If I'd known you in the distant days,
        The days now long since past
        When I fell in love
        So easily, so fast—

        If chance had sent one like you to love
        Instead of one untrue
        In my youthful prime,
        Once upon a time, oh!
        If I'd known you.

(*The last 16 bars of music are repeated*)
        If chance had sent one like you to love
        Instead of one untrue

Then I might have been
What is now a dream, oh!
If I'd Known You.

(*As the music ends,* Brazencourt *returns.* Squeezum *finishes writing, folds the letter, and brings it to Sotmore*)

Squeezum. This letter, sir, will release Captain Constant immediately.

Sotmore (*taking the letter and handing it to Brazencourt*) Let this letter be sent whither it is directed.

(Brazencourt *exits*)

(*Crossing to the table and uncorking the wine*) Come, honest Justice, and remember what you have promised to do every day of your life. (*He pours wine*) Come and pledge me; if thou leavest one drop in the glass thou shalt to gaol yet, by this bottle. (*He brings two full glasses, and hands one to Squeezum*)

Squeezum. I protest, sir, your hand is too bountiful. The wine will overcome me.

Sotmore (*crossing to Hilaret with the second glass*) I love to see a magistrate drunk. It is a glorious sight. Come, madam.

Hilaret (*taking the glass, but protesting*) Dear sir! I beg you would not compel me to it.

Sotmore (*returning to the table for his own glass*) By this bottle, but I will. Come, drink the Justice's health, as a token of amity. He is a good, honest, drunken fellow.

(Hilaret *and* Squeezum *each sip their wine*)

(*Draining his glass and putting it back on the table*) But let me give you a few words of wholesome advice. (*He moves down to Squeezum*)

(Hilaret *moves up to the table and puts down her glass, still almost full*)

Leave the girls to the boys, and stick to the bottle. It's more becoming to your years.

(Brazencourt *enters, followed by* Constant *and* Staff)

Brazencourt. Captain Constant is here, sir.

Constant (*moving to Hilaret and embracing her*) My Hilaret.

Hilaret. My Constant!

Sotmore. Give you joy, dear Captain, of your liberty!

Constant. Thank you, dear Sotmore; to you I am partly obliged for this. Ramble and I will give you six nights' drinking for it.

Sotmore. Where is Ramble? (*He knows full well, but can't resist a private joke with Constant, at Squeezum's expense*)

CONSTANT (*taking the cue and smiling*) Be not concerned for him. He's *very* safe. Fate has been kind to all of us.

KIND FATE   No. 18

(*As the music begins the grouping is* CONSTANT *with* HILARET, SOT-MORE *with* SQUEEZUM, BRAZENCOURT *with* STAFF. *These last two seem to be sharing a secret which gives them a smug satisfaction at the expense of the young lovers*)

CONSTANT (*singing*) Kind fate brought us together again,
                Kind fate.
                Never thought I would weather the pain,
                Kind fate.
                Just when I had lost faith in
                    My guiding star
                Just then destiny led me
                    To where you are

                Kind fate, what will the future bestow?
HILARET (*singing*)   Kind fate?
CONSTANT.   Joy or sadness, but one thing I know
HILARET.   Kind fate.
CONSTANT.   Our hearts no-one can sever,
                And I'll be grateful for ever,
                To kind, Kind Fate.

CONSTANT and HILARET (*together*)
                Kind fate brought us together again

SOTMORE and SQUEEZUM (*singing together*)
                Kind fate.

CONSTANT and HILARET (*together*)
                Never thought I would weather the pain

BRAZENCOURT and STAFF (*singing together, sardonically*)
                Kind fate!

CONSTANT.   Just when I had lost faith in
                    My guiding star.
HILARET.   Just then destiny led me
                    To where you are

ALL (*together*)   Kind fate, what will the future bestow,
                Kind fate?
                Joy or sadness, but one thing I know
                Kind fate.
                Our hearts no-one can sever,
                And I'll be grateful for ever
                To kind, Kind Fate.

(*As the music ends,* Squeezum *crosses to Staff*)

Squeezum. Mr Constable, do your duty.

Staff (*calling off*) Come in, there!

(*To the great glee of* Brazencourt, *the two* Watchmen *who had been concealed outside now enter*)

Squeezum. I charge you in the King's name, arrest these people.

(*The first* Watchman *takes charge of Constant and Hilaret, the second crosses to Sotmore and pushes him close to the others*)

I accuse that woman, and (*indicating Sotmore*) that man of conspiring to swear a rape against me.

Hilaret. You villain!

Sotmore. You rascal! Not even wine makes you honest.

Squeezum. Mr Constable, convey the prisoners to your house, where they will face a Justice. Away with them!

(*As they make their way from "The Tavern" to "Staff's House" where the trial is to be heard, the whole stage-level area is given the appearance of a courtroom. This can be most simply achieved by the cast slightly rearranging the existing furniture. Thus, the Seat of Justice for* Worthy *can be Squeezum's old desk, set at a new angle. The tavern table, set square, and with a chair at either end for the* Watchmen, *becomes the dock behind which stand the accused. The chairs from Politic's parlour can be moved forward for the witnesses,* Squeezum *and* Brazencourt. *This should be done as speedily as possible as the prisoners and their escorts remain on stage, marching to the trial, without making an exit*)

KIND FATE (*Reprise*)   No. 18A

Hilaret, Constant, Squeezum, Sotmore, Staff, Brazencourt,
The Watchmen (*singing together*)

> Kind fate

(*They march in silence for a bar*)

> Kind, kind fate!
> Kind fate.

(*Another bar*)

> Kind, kind fate!
> Kind fate.

(*And another*)

> Kind fate.

(*One more bar, taking them almost to their positions for the trial*)

> Kind, kind fate!

(*They have arrived.*

JUSTICE WORTHY *has arrived to hear the case.* BRAZENCOURT *takes one of the chairs reserved for witnesses,* SQUEEZUM *stands by the other.* HILARET, CONSTANT *and* SOTMORE *march straight behind the "dock" with a* WATCHMAN *on guard at either side.* STAFF *stands between the witnesses and the dock*)

SQUEEZUM (*in his best legal manner*) Brother Worthy, this is the woman I accuse, and this was the manner of it. I received a letter in an unknown hand, appointing me to meet at a tavern, and upon my arrival found this woman here alone, who after a short discourse, revealed herself to me in a most lascivious way. I—an unwilling witness of this rude exposure—felt it my duty to remain a closer observer. On a sudden she called out, "A rape, a rape!" Whereupon this man arrived (*he points to Sotmore*) and both together swore that if I did not instantly release (*pointing to Constant*) this fellow, with another whom I had already committed for notorious crimes, the woman would swear a rape against me. This I am ready to swear. (*He sits*)

WORTHY. What do you say to this, young woman?

HILARET. That I did threaten him I confess.

WORTHY. For what reason did you do this?

HILARET. Only to frighten him to discharge two gentlemen, whom he had villainously committed to custody.

WORTHY (*turning to Staff*) For what crime do they stand committed, Mr Constable?

STAFF. For rape, an't please your Worship.

SQUEEZUM (*standing*) Now, sir, let us proceed to show the character of this woman. (*Turning to the Innkeeper*) Brazencourt, what do you know of this . . . *fine* lady? (*He sits*)

BRAZENCOURT (*standing; he has always found perjury to Squeezum's instructions a profitable sideline*) I know nothing of her except that I kept her for half a year, till I was obliged to turn her off for stealing four of my shirts, two pairs of stockings, and a Prayer Book. (*He sits*)

HILARET. Sir, I beseech you to hear me . . .

WORTHY (*stopping her, sadly shaking his head*) I will never put confidence in an innocent countenance again. Well, woman, can you say anything for yourself?

HILARET. Oh! That I could hide myself for ever from this world! Oh, my Constant!

(FAITHFUL *enters, followed by* POLITIC, DABBLE *and* CLORIS)

SQUEEZUM. Come, sir, this is only wasting time. To gaol with the whole pack of them!

FAITHFUL (*bursting forward*) Hold, hold! (*He turns to Politic and indicates Hilaret in the dock*) Now, sir, will you believe your own eyes? Is not that your daughter?

POLITIC. It is indeed! Oh! My unfortunate daughter.

WORTHY. *Your* daughter, sir?

POLITIC. Yes, sir. *My* daughter, sir!

HILARET. My dear papa!

POLITIC. My poor child! That ever I should live to see thee come to such a pass.

WORTHY. Is it possible, Mr Politic, that this young lady is your daughter?

POLITIC. It is not only possible, sir, but true!

WORTHY (*with regret*) Nevertheless, the law must take its course. (*Firmly*) Away with them!

(RAMBLE, MRS SQUEEZUM *and* QUILL *enter*)

MRS SQUEEZUM. Where is the glory of the bench? This gallant Justice?

SQUEEZUM. Oh, my malignant stars!

MRS SQUEEZUM (*crossing to him, and producing a letter which she waves under his nose*) Do you know this hand, sir? Did you write this assignation? You are a noble gentleman truly, to make an appointment with a young woman to meet you in secret at a tavern!

WORTHY. What is the matter, Mrs Squeezum?

MRS SQUEEZUM (*crossing to him*) Mr Worthy, I am sure you will pity one who hath the misfortune to be married to a man who is as much a scandal to the commission he bears as you are an honour to it. My poor brain can no longer bear the burden of conniving at his rogueries. (*With an accusing finger pointed at her husband*) He, sir, he alone is guilty. And everyone else whom he hath accused is innocent.

SQUEEZUM (*rising and moving forward*) Harkye, madam, I shall be obliged to commit you to Bedlam, if you don't hold your tongue.

MRS SQUEEZUM. I shall prevent you in that, as well as in your other designs.

SQUEEZUM (*up to the Justice's desk*) Sir, I beseech you, hear no more!

WORTHY. That, sir, I cannot grant.

MRS SQUEEZUM (*handing the letter to Worthy*) Sir, I desire you would read that letter, which he sent (*indicating Hilaret*) to this young woman.

WORTHY (*reading*) "My little honeysuckle——"

SQUEEZUM (*turning away with a wince*) Oh, my unfortunate phraseology!

WORTHY. "——I will meet you within this half-hour at the *Eagle*. Enquire for Mr Jones. I hope, after what you have received from me today, you will not disappoint your Ever-Loving Bumble Bee."

(SQUEEZUM *looks as if he would like to sink into the floor*)

Did you write this letter, Mr Squeezum?

SQUEEZUM (*clutching at straws*) No, sir. I am ready to swear.

MRS SQUEEZUM. Sir, *I* will swear it *is* his hand.

FAITHFUL. And so will I.

QUILL (*his chance at last, after all these years*) And I brought it to the lady.

RAMBLE. Come, come, Justice. (*He moves towards Worthy's desk*) Thou hast proof enough of her innocence. I will give you my word she never intended more than to frighten him to the acquittal of Captain Constant here, whom he hath unjustly committed.

CLORIS (*recognizing his voice, and noticing him for the first time*) Ramble! It's my Ramble! (*She moves from the back of the "Court", where she has been standing with Dabble, to Ramble, who is standing in the well of the "Court". For the first time she is now in a position to see Brazencourt's face*)

RAMBLE. Oh, it is my Cloris! Once more restored to my despairing hopes.

CLORIS. What lucky stars have contrived this meeting?

RAMBLE. Very lucky stars they appear now, but they had a confounded ugly aspect some time ago.

(*As she embraces Ramble*, CLORIS *suddenly recognizes Brazencourt*)

CLORIS. Oh, villainy! Let that fellow be secured! He was the person from whose hands Captain Constant delivered me.

WORTHY. Secure him instantly.

(*The* WATCHMEN *move from the dock towards the witness chairs and carry out their orders*. HILARET, CONSTANT *and* SOTMORE, *now free, move from the dock to rejoin their friends*)

And secure that Justice, whom I shall no longer treat as a gentleman, but as his villainy has merited.

(SQUEEZUM *is arrested and placed beside Brazencourt*)

SQUEEZUM. Sir, you shall wish you had dealt more favourably with me.

WORTHY. Sir, your threatenings will not terrify me. Away with him.

MRS SQUEEZUM. And I'll follow him like his evil genius, till I have brought him to that justice he deserves.

I'LL BE THERE   No. 19

(*A suitable grouping for this number would be* RAMBLE, *with* CLORIS *and* DABBLE *down* R, STAFF, *with a* WATCHMAN *guarding* BRAZEN-

COURT *up* R, HILARET *and* CONSTANT *with* SOTMORE *up* L, WORTHY, *having climbed down from his desk, with* POLITIC, FAITHFUL *and* QUILL *down* L, SQUEEZUM *with his arresting* WATCHMAN C, *and* MRS SQUEEZUM *down* C)

MRS SQUEEZUM (*singing*)

> When in some dismal prison cell
> Your sins you must atone
> Console yourself with this, my love,
> You will not be alone.
>
> Like a ghost sent to plague you
> I'll be there.

ENSEMBLE (*singing*) She'll be there.

MRS SQUEEZUM.

> When you're most bent with ague
> I'll be there.

ENSEMBLE. She'll be there.

MRS SQUEEZUM.

> And it's no use you scheming
> To escape me when you're dreaming
> I'll be there—in your dreams—
> I'll be there

ENSEMBLE. She'll be there.

MRS SQUEEZUM.

> When you call for the warder
> I'll be there.

ENSEMBLE. She'll be there.

MRS SQUEEZUM.

> To install law and order
> I'll be there.

ENSEMBLE. She'll be there

MRS SQUEEZUM.

> Should you prove your repentance
> And they then cut short your sentence
> I'll be there—with an axe—
> I'll be there.

ENSEMBLE. She'll be there.

MRS SQUEEZUM.

> I'll be there all dressed up
> In my Sunday best
> And you'll hear me cheering
> Louder than the rest
>
> When the fiends first torment you
> I'll be there

ENSEMBLE. She'll be there.

MRS SQUEEZUM.

> When their tweezers have bent you
> I'll be there.

ENSEMBLE.   She'll be there.

MRS SQUEEZUM.   Should they run short of fuel
Or grow tired of being cruel
I'll be there—on the job—
I'll be there.

ENSEMBLE.   She'll be there all dressed up
In her Sunday best
And you'll hear her cheering
Louder than the rest

MRS SQUEEZUM.   When to Old Nick you grovel
I'll be there.

ENSEMBLE.   She'll be there.

MRS SQUEEZUM.   With my own little shovel,
I'll be there.

ENSEMBLE.   She'll be there.

MRS SQUEEZUM.   Should you go somewhere sweeter
And expect to find St Peter—
I'll be there,
At the gates,

EVERYBODY (*together*)
I'll
She'll   be there!

(*As the music ends,* SQUEEZUM *and* BRAZENCOURT *are marched out by the* TWO WATCHMEN, *and* MRS SQUEEZUM *follows*)

RAMBLE. My dear Cloris, I am so overjoyed at this unexpected meeting that I do not ask for the safety of our treasure.

CLORIS. It is as well you don't, because it's at the bottom of the ocean.

WORTHY. Mr Politic, I am heartily concerned at this misfortune which has befallen your daughter.

RAMBLE (*crossing*) Mr Politic? By heavens! Mr Politic? Had you not a son, sir, once?

POLITIC. Yes, sir, I had. But I turned him out of doors and believe he was hanged long ago.

RAMBLE. Then I am his ghost, just returned from the Indies.

(HILARET *reacts to this news and moves down stage, bringing* CONSTANT *with her, to join the family group.* POLITIC *is almost dumb-struck*)

When you turned me out of doors I joined a ship, changing my name to escape discovery—Father! (*They embrace*)

HILARET. Brother!

RAMBLE (*turning*) Sister! (*Suddenly it strikes him how nearly they come of having quite a different relationship, and he claps a hand to his mouth*)

WORTHY. Mr Politic, I rejoice in the reunion of your family.

RAMBLE. Well, Father, I have nothing more to ask of you, except for you to give your blessing not only to me but to my friend, Captain Constant, whose love I am certain will complete the happiness of my sister.

(*As* HILARET *brings* CONSTANT *forward*, RAMBLE *returns to Cloris's side*)

HILARET. Please, Papa!

WORTHY (*to Politic*) Sir, I do not think your children could be better disposed of.

POLITIC (*after a pause*) Let me see you all embrace one another.

EPILOGUE   No. 20

(*As* CONSTANT *kisses* HILARET, *and* RAMBLE *kisses* CLORIS, MRS SQUEEZUM *enters, followed by* SQUEEZUM, BRAZENCOURT *and the* TWO WATCHMEN)

MRS SQUEEZUM (*addressing the audience*)
      At length the dreadful hurricane is ended
      And I and spouse are safe together landed
      For after all this mighty fuss about it
      Our play has ended modestly, without it.

SQUEEZUM.   But, ladies, did not you too sympathize?
      Hey? Pray, confess, do all your frowns arise
      Because so much of Rape and Rape we bawl?
      Or is it that we have no Rape at all?

MRS SQUEEZUM.   Indeed, our Poet, to oblige the age,
      Had brought a dreadful scene upon the stage.
      But I, perceiving what his muse would drive at,
      Told him the ladies never would connive at
      A downright, actual Rape—unless in private!

SQUEEZUM.   So may no fears of such a fate affright
      The beauteous, kind spectators of tonight.

MRS SQUEEZUM.   Safe to your husbands' arms may you escape,
      And never know that dreadful thing, a Rape.

FINALE: LOCK UP YOUR DAUGHTERS   No. 21
(*Reprise*)

ENSEMBLE.   Lock Up Your Daughters!
      Here comes a rake!
      Lock Up Your Daughters!

Their chastity's at stake!
Here is a man with one thought in his head
Whom can I court and escort into bed?
Go round and knock up
The locksmith to lock up
Your daughters now!

Lock Up Your Daughters!
Spring's in the air.
Lock Up Your Daughters!
For wedding rings are rare.
You'd be amazed at the things they can delve
Into if they are not in bed by twelve.
Wind ev'ry clock up,
And you'd better lock up
Your daughters now!

Lock Up Your Daughters!
Don't set them free.
Lock Up Your Daughters!

RAMBLE.   But cut a key for me!

ENSEMBLE.   Virgins are treasures young men understand
'Til they've the patience to ask for her hand
Fathers . . . !
Lock Up Your Daughters Now!

PRODUCER'S NOTE

One of the delights of *Lock Up Your Daughters* is that there is no one "correct" way to stage it. To an unusual degree each producer is free to express his own creative ability, bound only by such facilities as are offered on the stage he is to use, and the resourcefulness of his scenic designer and stage crew.

Accordingly, this acting edition describes a simple, basic production, played without scene changes in a permanent composite setting.

The only essential requirements are five acting areas representing: (1) Politic's parlour, (2) Hilaret's bedroom, (3) Justice Squeezum's room, (4) Mrs Squeezum's boudoir, and (5) an area c stage, where all other scenes are played. Each area contains furniture and properties suitable to its location, and a list of these appears on pp. 67–68. If areas (2) and (4) can be set on rostrums, to suggest that they are on the first floors of their respective houses, so much the better.

A typical ground plan might look like this:

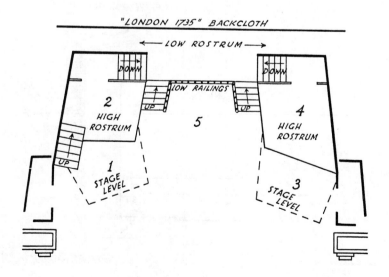

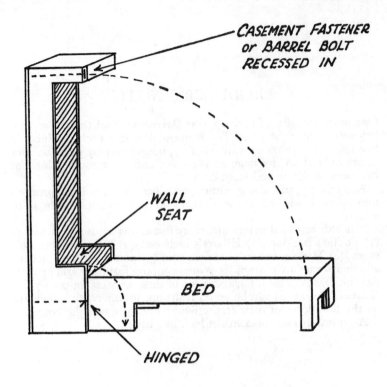

CASEMENT FASTENER or BARREL BOLT RECESSED IN

WALL SEAT

BED

HINGED

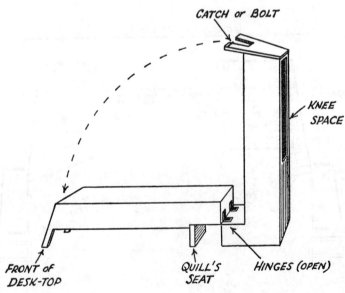

CATCH or BOLT

KNEE SPACE

FRONT of DESK-TOP

QUILL'S SEAT

HINGES (OPEN)

PROPERTIES AND FURNITURE PLOT

On stage: *Area 1*   Table. *On it:* a pile of newspapers
                            2 chairs

           Area 2   Dressing-table. *On it:* dressing (beauty jars and bottles),
                            a hand mirror
                            Stool

           Area 3   Trick desk (see plan on page 66) *On it:* ledger, quill pens,
                            inkwell, wig-stand, leather pouch containing coins
                            High stool

           Area 4   Dressing-table. *On it:* dressing (jars, bottles, powder
                            puff), a glass of cherry brandy
                            Stool
                            Wall seat, concealing trick bed (see plan on page 66)
           Area 5
               "*The Tavern*"
                    Rough table. *On it:* bottle of wine, 2 drinking vessels
                    2 chairs

               "*The Cell*"
                    Table
                    3 chairs

               "*Upstairs at the Eagle*"
                    Table. *On it:* bottle of wine, 2 glasses
                    2 chairs
                    Screen
                    Mirror

               "*The Trial Scene*"
                    A "dock"
                    2 witnesses' chairs
                    Justice's desk

Personal: (Act I)
           STAFF: A lantern on a pole
           POLITIC: 2 newspapers (later; a bundle of newspapers)
           CLORIS: Clothing, to pack into Hilaret's going-away bag
           DABBLE: A newspaper,
                        Pipe and tobacco
           BRAZENCOURT: Bottle of wine (for Sotmore)
           SQUEEZUM: Purse in pocket (for Hilaret)

Personal: (Act II)
           STAFF: Mrs Squeezum's letter to Ramble

CONSTANT: Squeezum's letter to Hilaret
FAITHFUL: ear trumpet
BRAZENCOURT: Tray. *On it:* quill pen, inkwell, paper, bottle of
        wine, 3 glasses
MRS SQUEEZUM: Squeezum's letter to Hilaret

Character costumes and wigs used in the performance of plays contained in
French's Acting Edition may be obtained from Messrs CHARLES H. FOX LTD,
184 High Holborn, London, W.C.1.

GENERAL LIGHTING PLOT

This basic plot assumes that Acting Areas 1 to 5 can be lit independently, and that three Battens for general lighting are also available, No. 1 to light the downstage area, No. 2 at mid stage, and No. 3 to light the backcloth. All this lighting should operate on dimmers.

Two Following Spots are required and their Plots are printed separately.

ACT I

Cue 1	As the OVERTURE ends	(Page 1)
	Batten No. 3 up to ¼	
Cue 2	STAFF moves to Area 3	(Page 1)
	Area 3 lighting up to FULL	
Cue 3	STAFF: "Evening, Mr Squeezum . . . (*Sings* All's Well"	(Page 1)
	Area 3 lighting dim OUT	
Cue 4	STAFF moves to Area 4	(Page 1)
	Area 4 lighting up to FULL	
Cue 5	STAFF: "I look divine tonight, and . . . (*Sings*) All's Well"	(Page 2)
	Area 4 lighting dim OUT	
Cue 6	STAFF moves above Area 5	(Page 2)
	Area 5 lighting up to FULL	
Cue 7	STAFF: "or under the table; either way . . . (*Sings*) All's Well"	(Page 2)
	Area 5 lighting dim OUT	
Cue 8	STAFF: "no good telling him . . . (*Sings*) All's Well"	(Page 2)
	Area 1 lighting up to FULL	
Cue 9	STAFF crosses C	(Page 2)
	Area 1 lighting dim OUT	
	Area 2 lighting up to FULL	
Cue 10	STAFF: "she thinks he is . . . (*Sings*) All's Well"	(Page 2)
	Area 2 lighting dim OUT	
Cue 11	STAFF (*singing*) "Nine o'clock on a fine summer's night"	(Page 2)
	Batten No. 3 dim OUT	
Cue 12	When STAFF is off stage	(Page 2)
	Area 2 lighting snap up FULL	
Cue 13	CLORIS: "all the good gifts of nature"	(Page 3)
	Batten No. 1 up to FULL	
	Area 2 lighting dim to ½	

Cue 14   End of "A Proper Man"   (Page 4)
               Area 2 lighting up to FULL
               Batten No. 1 dim OUT

Cue 15   POLITIC: "the expense of sailing 'em"   (Page 5)
               Area 1 begin slow build-up to FULL
               Batten No. 3 up to ¼

Cue 16   HILARET and CLORIS leave bedroom   (Page 6)
               Area 2 dim to ¼

Cue 17   POLITIC: "I cannot rest for these preparations"   (Page 6)
               Area 1 complete build-up to FULL *(from Cue 15)*
               Batten No. 3 dim OUT

Cue 18   POLITIC: "the loss of twenty daughters"   (Page 8)
               Battens No. 1 and No. 2 begin slow build-up to FULL
               Area 2 lighting dim OUT

Cue 19   POLITIC and DABBLE (*singing*) "of the rest—why
               fret?"   (Page 8)
               Battens No. 1 and No. 2 complete build-up to FULL *(from
               Cue 18)*

Cue 20   End of "It Must Be True"   (Page 10)
               Battens No. 1 and No. 2 dim OUT

Cue 21   POLITIC sits down   (Page 10)
               Area 1 quick dim OUT
               Area 5 lighting up to FULL

Cue 22   RAMBLE: "the ones I have already known"   (Page 11)
               Batten No. 1 up to ½

Cue 23   RAMBLE exits   (Page 13)
               Area 5 lighting dim OUT
               Batten No. 1 dim to ¼

Cue 24   HILARET enters   (Page 13)
               Batten No. 3 up to ¼

Cue 25   Start of " 'Tis Plain to See"   (Page 15)
               Batten No. 1 up to FULL

Cue 26   End of REPRISE of " 'Tis Plain to See"   (Page 18)
               Battens No. 1 and No. 3 snap OUT

Cue 27   When SQUEEZUM and QUILL in position   (Page 18)
               Area 3 lighting up to FULL

Cue 28   SQUEEZUM: "We must all take our chance, Quill"   (Page 19)
               Batten No. 1 up to ½

Cue 29   MRS SQUEEZUM exits   (Page 21)
               Area 3 lighting dim to ¼
               Batten No. 1 up to FULL

Cue 30   End of "On the Side"   (Page 22)
               Area 3 lighting up to FULL
               Batten No. 2 up to FULL

Cue 31	STAFF exits *Batten No. 2 fade* OUT *Batten No. 1 fade to* ¼ *Area 3 lighting fade to* ½	(Page 23)
Cue 32	SQUEEZUM: "Give us a kiss, eh?" *Area 4 lighting up to* ¾	(Page 24)
Cue 33	RAMBLE: "obliged to you, madam" *Area 3 lighting up to* ¾ *Area 4 lighting dim to* ¼	(Page 24)
Cue 34	HILARET: "humour the old devil a little" *Area 4 lighting up to* ¾ *Area 3 lighting dim to* ¼	(Page 24)
Cue 35	MRS SQUEEZUM: "the man you were reported to be"	(Page 24)
	Area 3 lighting up to ¾ *Area 4 lighting dim to* ¼	
Cue 36	SQUEEZUM: "teaching daughters to read and write" *Area 4 lighting up to* ¾ *Area 3 lighting dim to* ¼	(Page 25)
Cue 37	MRS SQUEEZUM: "you are charged withal" *Area 3 lighting up to* ¾ *Area 4 lighting dim to* ¼	(Page 25)
Cue 38	HILARET: "I fell a victim of their chaplain" *Area 4 lighting up to* ¾ *Area 3 lighting dim to* ¼	(Page 25)
Cue 39	RAMBLE: "trust yourself with me anywhere" *Area 3 lighting up to* ¾ *Area 4 lighting dim to* ¼	(Page 25)
Cue 40	SQUEEZUM: "beneath the burning glass' *Area 4 lighting up to* ¾	(Page 25)
Cue 41	HILARET: "Bumble bee" *Area 4 lighting dim* OUT *Area 3 lighting up to* FULL	(Page 26)
Cue 42	STAFF and RAMBLE exit *Battens No. 1 and No. 2 up to* FULL	(Page 27)
Cue 43	End of "When Does the Ravishing Begin?" *Area 3 lighting, and Battens No. 1 and No. 2 snap* BLACK- OUT	(Page 29)
Cue 44	When POLITIC and WORTHY in position *Area 1 lighting up to* FULL	(Page 29)
Cue 45	WORTHY: "from the Turks I cannot" *Area 2 lighting up to* ¼	(Page 30)
Cue 46	POLITIC: "compared with the news of the world?" *Area 1 lighting fade* OUT	(Page 30)
47	WORTHY: "all are lunatics" *Batten No. 3 up to* ¼	(Page 30)

Cue 48   HILARET reaches bedroom   (Page 30)
       Area 2 lighting up to FULL

Cue 49   CLORIS exits   (Page 31)
       Area 2 lighting dim OUT

Cue 50   CONSTANT: "What a comical turn of fate"   (Page 32)
       Batten No. 3 dim OUT
       Area 5 lighting up to ½

Cue 51   Start of "Lock Up Your Daughters"   (Page 34)
       Battens No. 1 and No. 2 up to FULL

Cue 52   End of "Lock Up Your Daughters"   (Page 35)
       Battens No. 1 and No. 2 dim to ¼
       Area 5 lighting up to FULL

Cue 53   Start of "Lovely Lover"   (Page 37)
       Batten No. 1 and No. 2 slow dim OUT
       Area 5 lighting slow dim OUT

ACT II

Cue 54   As the ENTR'ACTE ends   (Page 39)
       Area 3 lighting up to FULL

Cue 55   QUILL: "There's a plot afoot" (1st time)   (Page 40)
       Battens No. 1 and No. 2 up to ½
       Area 3 lighting dim OUT

Cue 56   End of "There's a Plot Afoot"   (Page 42)
       Battens No. 1 and No. 2 snap BLACK-OUT

Cue 57   When CONSTANT, RAMBLE and SOTMORE in position   (Page 42)
       Area 5 lighting up to FULL

Cue 58   CONSTANT: "And success attend you!"   (Page 43)
       Area 5 lighting dim OUT
       Area 4 lighting up to FULL

Cue 59   RAMBLE: "Now!"   (Page 44)
       Area 4 lighting snap BLACK-OUT

Cue 60   When POLITIC and DABBLE in position   (Page 44)
       Area 1 lighting up to FULL

Cue 61   Start of "It Must Be True" Reprise   (Page 46)
       Batten No. 1 up to FULL

Cue 62   POLITIC, DABBLE, FAITHFUL and CLORIS exit   (Page 46)
       Batten No. 1 and Area 1 lighting fade OUT

Cue 63   When MRS SQUEEZUM reaches stage level   (Page 46)
       Battens No. 1 and No. 2 very slowly build to FULL

Cue 64   End of "The Gentle Art of Seduction"   (Page 48)
       Battens No. 1 and No. 2 snap BLACK-OUT

Cue 65   When BRAZENCOURT and SERVING WENCH in position   (Page
       Area 5 lighting up FULL

Cue 66	Start of "Mister Jones"	(Page 48)
	Batten No. 1 up to ¾	
Cue 67	End of "Mister Jones"	(Page 50)
	Batten No. 1 dim OUT	
Cue 68	Start of "Sunny Sunday Morning"	(Page 51)
	Battens No. 1 and No. 2 up to FULL	
Cue 69	Start of "If I'd Known You"	(Page 54)
	Battens No. 1 and No. 2 dim to ½	
	Area 5 lighting to ½	
Cue 70	End of "If I'd Known You"	(Page 55)
	Area 5 lighting up to FULL	
Cue 71	WATCHMEN enter	(Page 57)
	Battens No. 1 and No. 2 up to FULL	
Cue 72	End of "Kind Fate" Reprise	(Page 58)
	Batten No. 3 up FULL	
	Areas 1, 3 and 5 lighting up FULL	

REMAIN TO END OF ACT II

PLOT FOR NUMBER 1 FOLLOWING SPOT

ACT I

To open: OFF

Cue 1	STAFF enters ON *Staff on his entrance, up* L, *and follow*	(Page 1)
Cue 2	STAFF (*whispering*) "Lock Up Your Daughters!" *Snap* OUT	(Page 2)
Cue 3	CLORIS: "All the good gifts of nature" ON *Hilaret and follow*	(Page 3)
Cue 4	POLITIC reaches Hilaret's bedroom *Snap* OUT	(Page 4)
Cue 5	DABBLE enters ON *Dabble on his entrance, and follow*	(Page 6)
Cue 6	DABBLE sits *Snap* OUT	(Page 6)
Cue 7	POLITIC: "the loss of twenty daughters" ON *Dabble and follow*	(Page 8)
Cue 8	DABBLE exits *Snap* OUT	(Page 10)
Cue 9	POLITIC sits, and Area 5 lighting up to FULL ON *Ramble and follow*	(Page 10)
Cue 10	RAMBLE exits *Snap* OUT	(Page 10)
Cue 11	RAMBLE re-enters ON *Ramble and follow*	(Page 10)
Cue 12	RAMBLE exits *Iris* OUT	(Page 13)
Cue 13	RAMBLE re-enters *Iris* IN *on Ramble and follow*	(Page 13)
Cue 14	End of " 'Tis Plain to See" *Snap* OUT	(Page 17)
Cue 15	STAFF enters ON *Staff and follow* (*iris in to cover the lantern*)	(Page 17)
Cue 16	End of REPRISE of " 'Tis Plain to See" *Iris* OUT *as Staff exits*	(Page 18)
Cue 17	MRS SQUEEZUM enters ON *Mrs Squeezum on her entrance and follow*	(Page 20)
Cue 18	MRS SQUEEZUM moves to beside MR SQUEEZUM TAKE IN *Mr Squeezum. Now follow him*	(Page 20)

Cue 19	End of "On the Side" *Snap* OUT	(Page 22)
Cue 20	Start of "When Does the Ravishing Begin?" ON *Mrs Squeezum and follow*	(Page 27)
Cue 21	End of "When Does the Ravishing Begin?" *Snap* OUT	(Page 29)
Cue 22	When POLITIC and WORTHY in position, and Area 1 lighting up to FULL ON *Politic and follow*	(Page 29)
Cue 23	POLITIC: "compared with the news of the world?" *Iris* OUT	(Page 30)
Cue 24	HILARET enters ON *Hilaret on her entrance and follow*	(Page 30)
Cue 25	End of "Lovely Lover" *Iris* OUT	(Page 32)
Cue 26	RAMBLE enters ON *Ramble on his entrance and follow*	(Page 32)
Cue 27	When RAMBLE moves to beside CONSTANT TAKE IN *Constant*	(Page 32)
Cue 28	HILARET moves to beside CONSTANT LEAVE *Constant*. PICK UP *Ramble and follow*	(Page 35)
Cue 29	RAMBLE exits *Snap* OUT	(Page 37)

ACT II

To open:	ON *Quill and follow*	(Page 39)
Cue 30	SQUEEZUM: "Do not anticipate" TAKE IN *Squeezum*	(Page 39)
Cue 31	SQUEEZUM exits STAY *with Quill*	(Page 39)
Cue 32	QUILL: "There's a plot afoot" (2nd time) *Snap* OUT	(Page 40)
Cue 33	HILARET enters ON *Hilaret on her entrance and follow*	(Page 40)
Cue 34	HILARET (*singing*) "He's got a plot" *Snap* OUT	(Page 40)
Cue 35	FAITHFUL enters ON *Faithful on his entrance and follow*	(Page 41)
Cue 36	FAITHFUL: "my young mistress" *Snap* OUT	(Page 41)
Cue 37	STAFF enters ON *Staff on his entrance and follow*	(Page 42)
Cue 38	STAFF exits *Snap* OUT	(Page 42)

REMAIN TO END OF ACT II

PLOT FOR NUMBER 2 FOLLOWING SPOT

ACT I

To open: OFF

Cue 1	YOUNG GALLANT enters ON *Young Gallant on his entrance, down* L, *and follow*	(Page 1)
Cue 2	YOUNG GALLANT exits *Snap* OUT	(Page 1)
Cue 3	STAFF: "Yonder in the dark" *Iris* IN on *Young Man, down* L	(Page 2)
Cue 4	STAFF: "No good telling him . . . (*Sings*) All's Well" *Iris* OUT	(Page 2)
Cue 5	CLORIS moves to stage level ON *Cloris and follow*	(Page 4)
Cue 6	End of "A Proper Man" LEAVE *Cloris.* PICK UP *Politic and follow*	(Page 4)
Cue 7	POLITIC reaches Hilaret's bedroom *Snap* OUT	(Page 4)
Cue 8	POLITIC: "the loss of twenty daughters" ON *Politic and follow*	(Page 8)
Cue 9	POLITIC sits, and Area 1 lighting dims OUT *Iris* OUT	(Page 10)
Cue 10	SOTMORE moves to beside Ramble ON *Sotmore and follow*	(Page 10)
Cue 11	SOTMORE: "expect thee with impatience" *Iris* OUT	(Page 13)
Cue 12	HILARET enters *Iris* IN on *Hilaret and follow*	(Page 13)
Cue 13	End of " 'Tis Plain to See" *Snap* OUT	(Page 17)
Cue 14	When POLITIC and WORTHY in position, and Area 1 lighting up to FULL ON *Worthy and follow*	(Page 29)
Cue 15	WORTHY exits *Snap* OUT	(Page 30)
Cue 16	CLORIS exits ON *Constant,* C *stage, and follow*	(Page 31)
Cue 17	When RAMBLE moves to beside Constant, and Spot 1 takes in CONSTANT *Snap* OUT	(Page 32)

Cue 18	SOTMORE enters ON *Sotmore and follow*	(Page 33)
Cue 19	HILARET enters LEAVE *Sotmore.* PICK UP *Hilaret and follow*	(Page 35)
Cue 20	HILARET moves to beside Constant TAKE IN *Constant*	(Page 35)
Cue 21	End of "Lovely Lover" *Iris* OUT *with last sung note*	(Page 38)

ACT II

To open: OFF

Cue 22	SQUEEZUM enters ON *Squeezum and follow*	(Page 40)
Cue 23	SQUEEZUM: "Favours I will win" *Snap* OUT	(Page 40)
Cue 24	POLITIC and DABBLE enter ON *Politic and Dabble and follow*	(Page 40)
Cue 25	POLITIC and DABBLE: "There's a pretty plot afoot"	(Page 41)
	Snap OUT	
Cue 26	MRS SQUEEZUM enters ON *Mrs Squeezum and follow*	(Page 41)
Cue 27	MRS SQUEEZUM: "And deposit all my heart" *Snap* OUT	(Page 41)
Cue 28	CONSTANT: "and success attend you" ON *Mrs Squeezum and follow*	(Page 43)
Cue 29	RAMBLE: "Now!" *Snap* OUT	(Page 44)
Cue 30	HILARET and SOTMORE enter ON *Hilaret on her entrance and follow*	(Page 50)
Cue 31	When SQUEEZUM moves to beside Hilaret TAKE IN *Squeezum. Now follow him*	(Page 52)
Cue 32	When SQUEEZUM moves to beside Sotmore TAKE IN *Sotmore*	(Page 53)
Cue 33	When SOTMORE crosses to Hilaret, and No. 1 spot takes in Sotmore STAY *with Squeezum*	(Page 53)
Cue 34	SOTMORE sets chair for Hilaret LEAVE *Squeezum.* PICK UP *Hilaret and follow*	(Page 54)
Cue 35	Start of "If I'd Known You" *Iris* OUT	(Page 54)
Cue 36	End of "Kind Fate" (1st time) ON *Squeezum and follow*	(Page 56)

Cue 37   SQUEEZUM: "Away with them!"   (Page 57)
             Snap OUT
Cue 38   MRS SQUEEZUM enters   (Page 63)
             ON *Squeezum and follow*

REMAIN TO END OF ACT II

BERNARD MILES, C.B.E.—*Actor, Director, Writer*

Educated at Uxbridge County School and Pembroke College Oxford, formerly a school teacher; made his first appearance on the stage at the New Theatre in 1930 as the 2nd Messenger in *Richard III*.

Founder, with his wife, of the Mermaid Theatre, an Elizabethan styled playhouse, first season 1951 and opened the Mermaid Theatre on Puddle Dock in 1959 with the Musical play *Lock Up Your Daughters* (which he also adapted from Henry Fielding's *Rape Upon Rape*). This was followed with his adaptation of *Treasure Island*, in which he played LONG JOHN SILVER.

Mr. Miles is co-author of the screenplay of *Thunder Rock* and *The Guinea Pig*, and co-author and co-director of *Tawny Pipit* in which he also played the lead.

LIONEL BART—*Composer, Lyricist and Playwright*

Lionel Bart began his professional career at the Theatre Royal, Stratford East in February 1959, writing the lyrics and music for *Fings Ain't Wot They Used T'Be*. In the same year there followed *Lock Up Your Daughters*, for which he wrote the lyrics, and *Oliver!* In 1960 came *Blitz*. For all three of the last named musicals he won an Ivor Novello Award and *Oliver!* was also a New York hit for which he received an Antionette Perry Award for the Best Musical of 1963. Mr Bart has composed several film scores including that for *The Tommy Steele Story*, and title songs, notably that for the film *From Russia With Love*. *Maggie May* and *Twang* are his most recent musical play successes.

LAURIE JOHNSON—*Composer and Conductor*

Laurie Johnson studied at The Royal College of Music. In his career as a composer and conductor he has written the scores for more than 20 feature films including *Tiger Bay*, H G Wells's *First Men in the Moon* and *Dr Strangelove*, and for 52 films on TV, the most famous of which is perhaps *The Avengers* theme music. He composed the music for *Pieces of Eight* together with Peter Cook and won the Award for the Best Score of 1959 with *Lock Up Your Daughters*. In 1967 he formed an association with lyricist Herbert Kretzmer, author Michael Pertwee, and director Peter Coe to produce the Musical *The Three Musketeers*.

MADE AND PRINTED IN GREAT BRITAIN BY
LATIMER TREND AND CO. LTD, WHITSTABLE
MADE IN ENGLAND